california pizza kitchen

family
cookbook

LARRY FLAX and RICK ROSENFIELD

PHOTOGRAPHY BY LUCY SCHAEFFER

WILEY

John Wiley & Sons, Inc.

This book is printed on acid-free paper.

Photography Copyright © 2008 by Lucy Schaeffer, except for pages 3 and 85.
Photograph on page 3 courtesy of California Pizza Kitchen.
Photograph on page 85 courtesy of Berliner Photography.
Published by John Wiley & Sons, Inc., Hoboken, New Jersey
Published simultaneously in Canada

For general information on our other products and services or for technical support, please contact our Customer Care Department within the United States at (800) 762-2974, outside the United States at (317) 572-3993 or fax (317) 572-4002.

Wiley also publishes its books in a variety of electronic formats. Some content that appears in print may not be available in electronic books. For more information about Wiley products, visit our web site at www.wiley.com.

Design by Elizabeth Van Itallie
Food styling by Jamie Kimm
Prop styling by Anna Last

Library of Congress Cataloging-in-Publication Data:

Flax, Larry.
  The California Pizza Kitchen family cookbook / Larry Flax and Rick Rosenfield ; photography by Lucy Schaeffer.
     p. cm.
  Includes index.
  ISBN 978-0-470-22939-2 (cloth : alk. paper)
 1. Pizza. 2. Cookery (Pasta). 3. California Pizza Kitchen. I. Rosenfield, Rick. II. California Pizza Kitchen. III. Title.
  TX770.P58F585 2008
  641.8'248--dc22

                          2007050140

Printed in China
10 9 8 7 6 5 4 3 2 1

We gratefully dedicate this book to our wives, Joni and Esther, whose unfailing support sustains us; to Peter, Michelle, Alex, and Avery Gillette, for helping us understand what kids like and want; to Rose Flax, who continues to be Larry's biggest fan; to Rick's children Ian, Nicole, and Dana, who grew up with CPK and shared in the joys; to Ian and his wife, Susanne, and their son, Largo, the newest member of the family; and to all the friends and family members who remain unconditionally supportive and committed to us and our causes. We could not do this without you.

contents

acknowledgments

It takes literally thousands of people to run a chain of successful restaurants, and believe it or not, each of them had a part in this book. The employees at our restaurants not only offer outstanding service to our customers but they also keep us on top of everything by getting back to us with customer feedback and ideas. For that, we are eternally grateful.

We would also like to thank our Senior Vice President of Culinary Development, Brian Sullivan, who magically translates our ideas into the dishes you all enjoy at our restaurants.

Thank you to Sarah Grover, Senior Vice President of Marketing and Public Relations, who has been with us from almost the start and without whom this book simply would not exist. And, to Erin Murphy, our Manager of Public Relations, who stayed on top of everyone, making sure that all of the elements came together.

If a picture is worth a thousand words, photographer Lucy Schaeffer is worth her weight in gold. Everyone loves to see photos in a cookbook, and ours are outstanding.

Last, but certainly not least, we wish to thank Justin Schwartz, our editor at Wiley & Sons, who managed to translate our vision for a family cookbook into this very accessible cookbook.

introduction

From the time we published our first cookbook in 1996, and probably from the time we opened the doors of the first CPK in 1985, we've known that a family cookbook was in our future. Our customers have always included families; that was our hope from the start. And, some of our toughest critics—and greatest inspirations—have been the kids. It was completely logical, then, to write a cookbook that would serve the whole family, from sophisticated, well-traveled adults, to teens going off to college, to the little ones, whose first solid food may well have been pizza.

Our goal with this book is threefold. First, we want to make our favorite—and your favorite—CPK specialties accessible to the whole family at home. We love to cook with our families. We may be in the restaurant business, but our grandkids are not. So, we've taken care to make sure that all of the recipes in this book can be executed by anyone, regardless of age or culinary skill. Sure, there are some tasks that should be carried out by adults. That's why it's a family cookbook!

Second, but just as important, we want to inspire the whole family to create their own pizzas, panini, salads, and desserts. All of our pizzas came about after a good deal of experimentation. That's really the name of the game. Take a risk. Try new combinations. Use our crusts and techniques and make the toppings your own. There's no right or wrong! And, when you come up with something you really love, be sure to let us know. As we already said, you inspire us, too!

Third, we believe that a family should cook and eat together. We already know that people love to congregate in the kitchen. Whether it's because of the enticing smells or the anticipation of a great meal, that's where people like to be. Preparing CPK dishes has the added appeal of allowing all of the participants to be creative. This isn't work, it's fun!

Over the years, tastes have changed, diets have come and gone, but one thing remains constant: people love our food. And some of our customers have literally grown up with us! Many of our customers started out with a Traditional Cheese Pizza or a bowl of Curly Mac & Cheese. After a while, they may have graduated to the Thai Chicken Pizza. Now, they're off to college and wondering how they can make a Chipotle Chicken Pizza or a Grilled Chicken Pesto Panini in their first apartment. Some are even wondering how they can make that same traditional CPKids' Mushroom, Pepperoni, and Sausage Pizza that they grew up with for their own kids.

Speaking of CPKids, and we often do, we run kitchen tours with them and we always, always listen to what they have to say. We truly believe that they are our future. Kids love to get into the kitchen and do their own thing. This cookbook is for them.

We are so thrilled to be a part of this evolution, and we are equally thrilled that you, our customers, have been a part of ours. So, we offer you this cookbook in the hope that the evolution will continue, in our house and yours.

Larry S. Flax   Rick Rosenfield

tools of the trade, and safety tips, too

Pizza is not fancy food, and making pizza at home does not require many specialized tools. Here are a few tools, though, that will help make your homemade pizza better and more fun to make. Be sure to follow the safety tips so that your pizza-making experiences will always leave fond family memories.

tools

Making pizza at home is fun and easy, especially when you have the right tools. Here are a few that we recommend.

• Pizza Cutter: The classic rolling pizza cutter certainly does the trick when it comes to cutting pizza into slices. You can also use a long, heavy chef's knife, or even a two-handled cheese knife. Be sure to transfer your pizza to a cutting board; don't cut directly on your pizza peel.

• Pizza Stone: The pizza stone is absolutely essential for a creating a crisp crust that bakes quickly. Make sure to "season" the stone (according to manufacturer's instructions) before using it.

• Pizza Peel: The best way to transfer your dressed pizza from the counter to a pizza stone is with a large pizza peel (sort of a giant spatula), and the best way to transfer it without any sticking is with a wooden peel. The wooden peel also cools quickly and won't cause a new piece of dough to rise if you've just taken another pizza out of the oven with the same peel (a metal pizza peel will continue to conduct heat).

• Electric Stand Mixer with Dough Hook: While this type of mixer can make all kinds of cooking easier, it is good for pizza dough only when you are making a large batch. If the batch is too small the dough will simply flop around the bowl without kneading. For small batches, use the paddle attachment on your mixer. But, remember, nothing beats the fun of kneading dough by hand, so get in there!

kitchen safety

You already know not to run around the kitchen with a knife in your hand. Here are a few other kitchen safety tips that you might not know:

• Always cool food completely before covering it and storing in the refrigerator.

• Thoroughly wash and sanitize your cutting boards, especially after cutting raw meats and raw chicken. Use a dishwasher-safe cutting board for cutting up chicken.

• Keep a hand sanitizer in your kitchen and always use it after handling raw chicken.

• Keep sanitizer wipes handy for cleaning countertops and other work surfaces. Don't use the same wipe for a large surface or for cleaning multiple surfaces—this will just spread the germs around.

• Keep raw chicken refrigerated and take it out just before cooking.

• Keep your knives sharp, and teach your kids how to use them properly. If a cut happens, it will be "cleaner" with a sharp knife.

• Always apply first aid immediately to cuts and burns.

the basics

Great pizza always starts with great dough. If the dough is prepared properly, there's virtually no limit to what can go on top. That's where your own creativity comes in! Here are our dough recipes, along with basic sauces and various chicken preparations. The rest is up to your imagination!

traditional pizza dough

Makes 1 pound—enough for one 13-inch pizza, two 9-inch pizzas, or four 6-inch pizzas

Make your own pizza dough when you have plenty of time to let it rise and fully develop its flavor. But if you do not have the time, you can still make fabulous pizzas using storebought doughs and crusts. This recipe can easily be doubled, or even tripled for a pizza party. You can use the dough hook attachment on your stand mixer if you're making a double or quadruple batch of this dough.

SHOPPING/PANTRY/REFRIGERATOR LIST	HOW MUCH YOU'LL NEED
• Active dry yeast (not "quick rise" type)	1 teaspoon
• Warm water (105° to 110°F)	1 cup + 1 tablespoon
• Unbleached bread or all-purpose flour	2½ cups
• Sugar	2 teaspoons
• Kosher salt	1 teaspoon
• Extra-virgin olive oil	1 tablespoon + 1 teaspoon

SPECIAL EQUIPMENT

Stand mixer with paddle attachment or food processor with plastic blade (both optional); do not use a hand-held mixer, which may shred the dough

PREPARATION

1 In a small bowl, dissolve the yeast in the water. Make sure the water is not too hot, as this will kill the yeast and prevent the dough from rising.

2 *If using a stand mixer,* use the paddle because the dough hook will not mix this size batch efficiently. In the mixing bowl, combine the flour, sugar, salt, and 1 tablespoon of the olive oil and stir by hand just to distribute. Add the dissolved yeast and place the bowl and paddle on the mixer. Start mixing on the lowest speed to mix. Increase the speed slightly and mix for 2 to 3 minutes,

until the dough is smooth and elastic. Do not over-knead, as this will build up too much gluten and make the dough difficult to shape.

If using a food processor, be sure to use the plastic blade; the metal knife will cut through the gluten strands and keep the dough from developing any "body." Proceed as for the stand mixer, making sure to stop kneading as soon as the dough forms a smooth ball. Over-kneading could overheat the dough because the mixing bowl is directly above the motor.

If mixing by hand, place the dry ingredients in a 4- to 6- quart mixing bowl, and stir to combine. Make a well in the middle and pour the liquids, reserving 1 teaspoon of olive oil. Use a wooden spoon to combine the ingredients. Once all the flour is mixed in, turn the dough onto a lightly floured work surface and, with lightly oiled hands, knead the dough for 5 minutes. It should be smooth and elastic, but will still be slightly sticky.

3 Place the remaining teaspoon of oil in a 1-quart mixing bowl and spread it with your fingertips. Place the dough ball in the bowl, move it around the oil, then turn it over so that the oiled side is facing upward. Cover the bowl tightly with plastic wrap and allow the dough to rise until doubled in bulk, 1½ to 2 hours.

4 You may use the dough at this point, but if possible—and this requires some planning—punch the dough down, re-shape it into a ball, and cover tightly with plastic wrap. Refrigerate the dough overnight; this will develop a more flavorful dough with a chewier consistency.

5 About 2 hours before you are ready to assemble your pizza, remove the dough from the refrigerator. If making individual pizzas, use a sharp knife to divide the dough into 2 or 4 equal portions.

6 Roll each portion of dough into a round ball on a smooth, clean surface, making sure to seal any holes by pinching or rolling.

7 Place the newly formed dough balls in a glass baking dish, spaced far enough apart to allow for each to double in size. Seal the top of the dish with clear plastic wrap. Set aside at room temperature until the dough balls have doubled in size, about 2 hours. They should be smooth and puffy. Dress the pizza according to the recipe.

neapolitan (thin crust) pizza dough

Makes about 14 ounces—enough for one 14-inch pizza or two 10-inch pizzas

Thin and crisp when baked, this is the pizza dough of southern Italy. It is also perfect for our Dessert Pizzas (pages 104 to 105). The toppings on this pizza should be thinly sliced and lighter in weight than those used on our Traditional Pizza Dough (page 14).

SHOPPING/PANTRY/REFRIGERATOR LIST	HOW MUCH YOU'LL NEED
• Active dry yeast (not "quick rise" type)	1 teaspoon
• Warm water (105° to 110°F)	$^3/_4$ cup + 1$^1/_2$ tablespoons
• Unbleached bread or all-purpose flour	1$^3/_4$ cups + extra for rolling
• Whole wheat flour	2 tablespoons
• Sugar	1 teaspoon
• Kosher salt	1 teaspoon
• Extra-virgin olive oil	2 teaspoons

SPECIAL EQUIPMENT
• Stand mixer with paddle attachment or food processor with plastic blade (both optional); do not use a hand-held mixer, which may shred the dough
• Wooden rolling pin (thicker in the middle, if you have one)

PREPARATION

1 Follow steps 1 through 3 for Traditional Pizza Dough, using 1 teaspoon of oil to make the dough and 1 teaspoon to grease it after mixing. Before letting the dough rise, divide it into 2 pieces, if desired, and form each piece into a ball. Let the dough rise on a greased cookie sheet, covered loosely with plastic wrap or a damp towel. The dough should take about 2 hours to double in bulk at room temperature.

2 To roll and shape the dough, lightly flour your hands and generously flour a clean, flat work surface. Work with 1 piece of dough at a time. Place it on the floured surface and press down with your fingertips in the middle, spreading the dough with your hands. When the dough has doubled in width, use a floured rolling pin to roll it very thin, like flatbread. The outside rim should be slightly thicker than the center of the dough.

3 Using a broad spatula, transfer the dough to a pizza peel. Don't worry about keeping a perfect circle; you can reshape the pizza once it is on the peel. Reshape the dough slightly, pinching together any holes that may have formed. Dress the pizza according to the recipe.

honey-wheat pizza dough

Makes 1 pound—enough for one 13-inch pizza, two 9-inch pizzas, or four 6-inch pizzas

Prepared in the same way as Traditional Pizza Dough, this one lends a sweet-nutty flavor that complements spicy toppings beautifully.

SHOPPING/PANTRY/REFRIGERATOR LIST
- Active dry yeast (not "quick rise" type)
- Warm water (105° to 110°F)
- Unbleached bread flour
- Whole wheat flour
- Clover honey
- Kosher salt
- Extra-virgin olive oil

HOW MUCH YOU'LL NEED
1 teaspoon
1 cup + 1 tablespoon
1 cup
$1\frac{1}{2}$ cups
1 tablespoon + 2 teaspoons
1 teaspoon
1 tablespoon + 1 teaspoon

SPECIAL EQUIPMENT
Stand mixer with paddle attachment or food processor with plastic blade (both optional); do not use a hand-held mixer, which may shred the dough

PREPARATION
Follow the directions for Traditional Pizza Dough (page 14).

stretching and shaping pizza dough

PREPARATION

1 Lightly dust a clean, smooth work surface that is at least 12 × 12 inches. Start with a room-temperature dough ball (see Traditional Pizza Dough, page 14), taking care to retain the round shape when transferring the dough to the floured work surface. Use your hand or a rolling pin to press the dough down, forming a flat circle about ½ inch thick. Pinch the dough between your fingers all around the edge of the circle, forming a lip or rim that rises about ¼ inch above the center surface of the dough. Continue this outward stretching motion of the hands until you have formed a 9-inch round of pizza dough.

2 To dress the pizza, lightly sprinkle cornmeal, semolina, or flour over the surface of a wooden pizza peel. Arrange the stretched dough over the dusted peel surface. Make sure that all of your pizza toppings are prepared and cooled. Working quickly to prevent the dough from getting soggy, top the dough according to the recipe.

3 When you are ready to transfer the pizza to the pizza stone in the preheated oven, grasp the handle of the peel and execute a very small test jerk to verify that the pizza will come easily off the peel. If the dough does not move freely, carefully lift the edges of the dough and try to rotate it by hand. Extreme cases may require that you toss more flour under the dough's edges.

4 Once the dough is moving easily on the peel, open the oven and position the edge of the peel over the center of the stone, about two-thirds from the front of the stone. Jiggle and tilt the peel to get the pizza to start sliding off. When the pizza begins to touch the stone, pull the peel quickly out from under it. Don't attempt to move the pizza until it has begun to set, about 3 minutes. The peel can be slid under the pizza to move or remove it.

5 While the pizza is baking, prepare another piece of dough, if you have one. Make sure, however, that you have a way to remove the baked pizza (e.g., a second peel or 2 broad spatulas) while the unbaked one sits on the peel. The peel must also be at room temperature before you place any raw dough on it.

marinara/pizza sauce

Makes 1 cup

If you don't have time to make your own sauce, don't let that stop you from making your own pizza! Use your favorite storebought marinara sauce, but thicken it a bit over medium heat so that it does not make the crust soggy. Be sure to cool any pizza sauce completely before using it on raw pizza dough.

SHOPPING/PANTRY/REFRIGERATOR LIST
- Olive oil
- Garlic
- Roma tomatoes
- Oregano
- Basil
- Kosher salt
- Ground black pepper
- Tomato paste

HOW MUCH YOU'LL NEED
1 tablespoon
2 teaspoons minced
2 large ($1/2$ pound)
1 teaspoon chopped fresh, or $1/2$ teaspoon dried
1 teaspoon chopped fresh, or $1/2$ teaspoon dried
$1/2$ teaspoon
Pinch
1 tablespoon

PREPARATION

1 Heat the olive oil in a small nonstick frying pan over medium heat. Do not allow it to smoke. Add the garlic and cook, stirring constantly, until it just begins to turn light brown, 1 to 2 minutes. Do not allow the garlic to burn, as it will make the sauce bitter.

2 Add the remaining sauce ingredients except the tomato paste, and stir well. Reduce the heat and simmer the sauce until all of the liquid evaporates, about 10 minutes. Stir in the tomato paste and cook for an addition 2 minutes. Remove from the heat and cool completely before using. Store covered in the refrigerator for up to 1 week.

VARIATION
Spicy Marinara Sauce: Double the amount of garlic and add $1/4$ teaspoon crushed red pepper flakes along with it. Roughly chop 2 fresh basil leaves and stir into the sauce after adding the tomato paste.

grilled chicken for salads, pizzas and panini

By simply changing the seasoning, you can use this method to grill chicken breasts for any of our dishes.

SHOPPING/PANTRY/REFRIGERATOR LIST	HOW MUCH YOU'LL NEED
• Boneless, skinless chicken breasts	2 pounds

For Grilled Garlic Chicken:

• Olive oil	6 tablespoons
• Garlic	2 tablespoons finely chopped
• Soy sauce	1 tablespoon
• Kosher salt	1½ teaspoons

For Grilled Greek Chicken:

• Olive oil	1 to 2 tablespoons
• Greek spice blend	¼ cup

For Grilled Jamaican Jerk Chicken:

• Olive oil	1 to 2 tablespoons
• Jamaican jerk seasoning blend	1 tablespoon + 1½ teaspoons
• Cayenne pepper (optional)	1½ teaspoons

SPECIAL EQUIPMENT
Meat mallet, meat thermometer

PREPARATION

1 Place the chicken breasts between sheets of waxed or parchment paper, and gently pound to a thickness of ½ inch. Do not pound them too thin; this is just to ensure that they will cook evenly.

2 Combine the olive oil and seasonings in a large mixing bowl. Stir to mix. Add the chicken breasts to the bowl, one by one, turning each in the marinade. Place the chicken in the refrigerator for 10 to 20 minutes.

3 If you have a hot grill available, grill the chicken for 3 to 4 minutes on each side. Do not overcook. If no grill is available, preheat the oven to 350° F and bake the chicken, skin side up in a pan, for about 30 minutes. The internal temperature should be 165° F.

4 Use the chicken immediately, as desired; or let it cool and refrigerate for up to 3 days.

appetizers, salads, and panini sandwiches

Any one of these recipes can be multiplied or divided to serve a couple or a crowd. Also, there's a lot of finger food here—the perfect excuse for both adults and kids to eat with their hands!

avocado club egg rolls

Makes 8 egg rolls (4 to 8 appetizer servings)

Everyone loves egg rolls, but they're just as much fun to make as they are to eat. It's really a family affair, where adults can do the chopping and frying, and the kids make the rolls. The best part is the combination of flavors and textures: creamy avocado, crisp bacon, garlicky grilled chicken, and melted cheese. Be sure to prepare these in the exact order written, to prevent the wrappers from becoming soggy. You can use your favorite ranch dressing to make the Ranchito Sauce for dipping.

SHOPPING/PANTRY/REFRIGERATOR LIST	HOW MUCH YOU'LL NEED
• Egg roll wrappers (6-inch square)	8
• Grilled Chicken (page 22)	1 breast, diced $^3/_8$ inch
• Roma tomatoes	2 large, seeded and diced $^1/_4$ inch
• Cooked bacon	$^1/_4$ cup chopped (1 to 2 strips)
• Monterey Jack cheese	2 ounces, grated ($^2/_3$ cup)
• Ripe Hass avocado	1 medium, peeled, pitted, and sliced
• Eggs	2 large
• Cold water	2 tablespoons
• Cornstarch	2 tablespoons
• Vegetable oil	2 to 3 cups
• Italian (flat-leaf) parsley	4 large sprigs
• Ranch dressing	$1^1/_4$ cups
• Mayonnaise	$^1/_4$ cup
• Hot sauce	1 tablespoon + $1^1/_2$ teaspoons

SPECIAL EQUIPMENT
$^1/_2$-inch pastry brush, candy or frying thermometer

PREPARATION

1 Place the egg roll wrappers on a flat, dry surface with one corner of each pointing toward you (i.e., as a diamond, not a square).

2 Distribute the chicken, tomatoes, bacon, and cheese on the wrappers in a row that is $1^1/_2$ to 2 inches wide and 5 inches long. Make sure that the filling is never less than 1 inch from the edge of the wrapper. Divide the avocado slices among the egg rolls, placing them on top of the cheese with the longer (skin) side toward you.

3 Stir the eggs in a small bowl to lightly liquify. Add 2 tablespoons of cold water and beat with a fork until evenly mixed.

4 Working with one egg roll at a time, lightly brush egg wash over ½ inch of each side of the wrapper. Fold the corner closest to you over the filling, pressing down and pulling tight toward the center. Press the left and right corners down to seal the edge. Lightly coat the 2 bottom corners with egg wash, then fold right and left corners inwards over the filling, pressing down to seal the edge. Add additional egg wash to the top corner creases and press down to seal. Continue rolling into a compact roll, pressing lightly to seal all edges.

5 Line a 9 × 13-inch baking dish with waxed or parchment paper. Sift half the cornstarch over the paper, and place the finished egg rolls in the dish, making sure they do not touch one another. If you're going to fry the egg rolls later, sift the remaining cornstarch over the egg rolls, cover with plastic wrap, and refrigerate for up to 24 hours.

6 Heat the oil to 375° F in a deep 10-inch skillet. Fry the egg rolls, making sure that they are not touching (you may have to do this in 2 batches), for about 1½ minutes. Turn with tongs, and fry for another 1 to 1½ minutes, or until the egg rolls are golden brown all over. Remove with tongs and drain completely on paper towels. Cut each egg roll in half diagonally and garnish each pair with a sprig of parsley.

7 Make Ranchito Sauce by whisking ½ cup of ranch dressing with the mayonnaise and hot sauce. Serve the egg rolls with the Ranchito Sauce in one bowl and the remaining ¾ cup ranch dressing in another bowl on the side for dipping.

lettuce wraps with chicken

Makes 4 appetizers (2 wraps each)

Think of these as Asian soft tacos, where the tortilla is replaced with a crisp let-tuce leaf. In traditional Chinese cuisine, the filling may be made of chicken or squab; at CPK we know that families love chicken. We also know that everyone likes to "build his or her own," and this is your chance to do just that. You can serve the components of these wraps on individual plates, or put them all in the middle of the table. If you have a lazy Susan, even better!

SHOPPING/PANTRY/REFRIGERATOR LIST	HOW MUCH YOU'LL NEED
• Canola oil	1 tablespoon + 1 teaspoon
• Minced or coarsely ground chicken	1 pound
• Water chestnuts (canned in water)	1 (five-ounce) can, drained and chopped
• Shiitake mushrooms	4 medium, stemmed and chopped
• Lettuce Wrap Sauce (recipe follows)	1 cup
• Scallions (green onions)	2, chopped (white and pale green parts only)
• Chili oil	1/2 teaspoon
• Crisp Rice Sticks (page 118)	2 cups
• Iceberg lettuce	8 outer leaves

SPECIAL EQUIPMENT
Wok, or very heavy frying pan

PREPARATION

1 Heat a wok over high heat. Add 1 tablespoon of the canola oil by drizzling it around the upper edge of the wok. Add the chicken in small pieces, crumbling it with a metal spoon as it cooks. Continue cooking until all of the chicken is broken apart and cooked through, 6 to 7 minutes. Drain the chicken in a large strainer or colander.

2 Replace the wok over the heat. Add the remaining canola oil and heat it thoroughly. Add the water chestnuts and mushrooms, and stir-fry for 30 seconds.

3 Add the chicken back to the wok and pour in 1/2 cup of the sauce. Cook for about 1 minute, until the liquid has been absorbed and the chicken has darkened in color. Add the scallions and chili oil, and stir-fry for about 15 seconds. Turn off heat.

4 Divide the rice sticks among 4 serving plates, then divide the chicken mixture among the plates, mounding it on top of the rice sticks. Stack the lettuce cups on a plate and place the remaining sauce in shallow dishes or ramekins for dipping. To serve, place a scoop of the chicken and rice sticks in each lettuce cup. Cup the leaf and dip in the sauce, then eat as you would a taco. Serve immediately.

LETTUCE WRAP SAUCE

Makes 1 cup

. . . .

SHOPPING/PANTRY/REFRIGERATOR LIST
- Cornstarch
- Water
- Seasoned rice vinegar
- Seasoned rice wine
- Soy sauce
- Asian sesame oil
- Sugar
- Garlic
- Fresh ginger

HOW MUCH YOU'LL NEED
$1/2$ teaspoon
$1^1/2$ teaspoons
2 tablespoons + 1 teaspoon
2 tablespoons + 2 teaspoons
$1/4$ cup
1 tablespoon + $1^1/2$ teaspoons
1 tablespoon + $3/4$ teaspoon
2 tablespoons finely minced
2 teaspoons finely minced

. . . .

PREPARATION

1 Stir together the cornstarch and water and set aside.

2 Pour the rice vinegar, rice wine, and soy sauce into a small pot. Stir in the cornstarch mixture, followed by the sesame oil and sugar. Cook this mixture over low heat until it just begins to simmer.

3 Add the garlic and ginger, and continue cooking, stirring constantly, for about 5 minutes.

4 Cool and use immediately, or refrigerate for up to 5 days.

SPICY VARIATION
Add your favorite hot sauce or chili paste to taste.

orange chicken lettuce wraps

Makes 4 appetizers (2 wraps each)

Knowing that Chinese orange chicken is a favorite among adults and kids alike, we decided to serve it like our Lettuce Wraps (page 27) for a dish that we can eat with our hands.

SHOPPING/PANTRY/REFRIGERATOR LIST	HOW MUCH YOU'LL NEED
• Canola oil	2 cups + 2 teaspoons
• Boneless, skinless chicken breast	8 ounces
• Milk	2 tablespoons
• Fine saltine cracker crumbs	$\frac{1}{4}$ cup
• All-purpose flour	$\frac{1}{4}$ cup
• Seasoned salt	$1\frac{1}{4}$ teaspoons
• Water chestnuts (canned in water)	1 (five-ounce) can, drained and chopped
• Shiitake mushrooms	4 medium, stemmed and chopped
• Carrot	1 large, peeled and cut into 2-inch long julienne
• Scallions (green onions)	1 bunch, chopped (white and pale green parts only)
• Szechuan Orange Sauce (recipe follows)	1 cup
• Crisp Rice Sticks (page 118)	2 cups
• Iceberg lettuce	8 outer leaves

SPECIAL EQUIPMENT

Wok, or very heavy frying pan, small pot for frying, candy or frying thermometer, wire skimmer

PREPARATION

1 Heat 2 cups of oil to 375° F in a small pot. Meanwhile, cut the chicken pieces into $\frac{1}{2}$-inch cubes and place them in a small mixing bowl. Stir in the milk.

2 Make sure that the cracker crumbs are evenly and finely crushed. Combine them with the flour and seasoned salt until evenly blended. Stir this coating mixture into the chicken pieces until all of the chicken is evenly coated and all of the liquid is absorbed.

3 Carefully add the chicken to the hot oil, avoiding any clumps of breading mixture. Fry for about 45 seconds; the chicken should be thoroughly cooked (remove 1 piece and cut in half to test). Remove the chicken with a wire skimmer and drain thoroughly on several layers of paper towels.

4 While the chicken is frying, heat a wok over high heat. Drizzle the remaining 2 teaspoons oil around the inside rim of the wok. Add the water chestnuts, mushrooms, carrot, and scallions to the wok and cook, stirring and tossing, for about 30 seconds. Add half the sauce and cook for an additional 15 seconds, stirring constantly. Add the drained chicken pieces to the wok and toss for about 10 seconds, making sure that all of the chicken is coated with sauce. Remove from the heat.

5 Divide the rice sticks among 4 plates, then top with the chicken mixture. Stack the lettuce cups on a plate and place the remaining sauce in shallow dishes or ramekins for dipping. To serve, place a scoop of the chicken and rice sticks in each lettuce cup. Dip in the sauce and eat as you would a taco.

SZECHUAN ORANGE SAUCE

Makes 1 cup

You'll find all of the ingredients for this tangy sauce in an Asian market or the Asian section of most supermarkets.

SHOPPING/PANTRY/REFRIGERATOR LIST	HOW MUCH YOU'LL NEED
• Orange juice concentrate	$1/4$ cup + $1 1/2$ teaspoons
• Sweet chili sauce	$3/4$ cup + 1 tablespoon
• Sweet soy sauce (*ketjap manis*)	$2 1/4$ teaspoons
• Soy sauce	2 teaspoons
• Seasoned rice vinegar	$1 3/4$ teaspoons
• Seasoned rice wine	$1 1/2$ teaspoons

PREPARATION

Whisk or blend all of the ingredients until smooth. Use immediately, or store in the refrigerator for up to 3 days. Whisk before using.

miso salad with crab and shrimp

Makes 4 entrées

Miso, or fermented soybean paste, is a traditional condiment in Japanese cooking. It has also become almost mainstream in Western cooking, where it is used to add a sweet-salty flavor and creamy texture to dishes. We thought it would work well in a dressing. In fact, it worked so well that we decided to create a whole salad around it! This salad also introduces a new Japanese vegetable to our menu: daikon, or Japanese white radish. The daikon adds a cool crunch and a great contrast to the dish.

SHOPPING/PANTRY/REFRIGERATOR LIST	HOW MUCH YOU'LL NEED
• Napa cabbage	1 head, cut into $1/2$-inch strips
• Red cabbage	1 small head, cored and chopped
• Carrots	2 large, peeled and julienned
• Daikon radish	1 small, peeled and julienned
• English (hothouse) cucumber	1 large, peeled, cored, and julienned
• Cooked shelled edamame (soybeans)	2 cups
• Miso Dressing (recipe follows)	$1^3/_4$ cups
• Fried Wonton Strips (page 118)	3 cups
• Crisp Rice Sticks (page 118)	2 cups
• Ripe Hass avocados (optional)	2, peeled, pitted and cut into $1/2$-inch dice
• Lump crab meat	$1/2$ pound, shredded
• Cooked shrimp	10 ounces, quartered (tails removed)
• Scallions (green onions)	4, thinly cut at an angle (white and pale green parts only)

SPECIAL EQUIPMENT
Squeeze bottle or syrup dispenser

PREPARATION

1 Place the cabbages, carrots, radish, cucumber, and edamame in a very large mixing bowl and toss to mix. Pour in 1 cup of dressing and toss, making sure that everything is evenly coated. Gently toss in the Fried Wonton Strips, Crisp Rice Sticks, and diced avocado.

2 Divide the salad among 4 very large, chilled serving plates. Top each with crab and shrimp. Place the remaining dressing in a squeeze bottle or syrup dispenser and drizzle over the salads. Garnish with scallions and serve.

MISO DRESSING
Makes about 1³/₄ cups

Miso, or fermented soybean paste, adds a wonderful salty-sweet flavor and lots of body to this creamy dressing. Choose a mild, light-colored miso, which is available in the refrigerator section of most better supermarkets.

SHOPPING/PANTRY/REFRIGERATOR LIST	HOW MUCH YOU'LL NEED
• Light yellow miso	¹/₂ cup
• Rice vinegar	¹/₃ cup
• Sugar	¹/₂ cup
• Egg Beaters or lightly beaten egg	2 teaspoons
• Kosher salt	³/₄ teaspoon
• Ground black pepper	Pinch
• Cold water	¹/₄ cup
• Soybean oil	³/₄ cup

PREPARATION
Place all of the ingredients except the oil and water in a blender or food processor. Add ¼ cup cold water and mix well. With the machine on, add the oil in a thin stream until it is completely incorporated. Use immediately, or refrigerate for up to 3 days. Mix well before using.

grilled vegetable salad

Makes 4 entrées

A good grilled vegetable salad, especially one with a great variety of perfectly cooked vegetables served on crisp greens, is a thing of beauty. We thought our customers would love the healthful, low-calorie option—and we were right!

SHOPPING/PANTRY/REFRIGERATOR LIST

- Romaine lettuce

- Frozen corn kernels, thawed
- Kosher salt
- Ground black pepper
- Sun-dried tomatoes in olive oil
- Grilled scallions, zucchini, Japanese eggplant, and asparagus (page 120)
- Balsamic vinaigrette dressing
- Ripe Hass avocados

Optional:
- Grilled Garlic Chicken (page 22)

HOW MUCH YOU'LL NEED

3 heads (or 3 six-ounce bags of chopped Romaine)

1 cup
pinch
pinch
8 halves or ½-cup julienne strips
2 cups each

1 cup
2, peeled, pitted, and sliced

4 breasts

PREPARATION

1 If using whole heads of romaine, remove the outer leaves and chop the remaining leaves into 1-inch pieces. Wash and spin dry. If using bagged romaine, chop coarsely. Place the salad in a large mixing bowl.

2 Heat a heavy frying pan over high heat. Place the corn kernels in the pan and roast them for about 10 minutes, stirring often. Remove from the heat and sprinkle with salt and pepper. Add the corn to the romaine.

3 Drain the sun-dried tomatoes well and cut halves into julienne strips. Add to the salad.

4 If the grilled vegetables are cold, microwave them for 1 to 2 minutes in a covered bowl. They should be heated, but not cooked any further. Add the vegetables to the romaine.

5 Pour in the dressing and toss to coat everything evenly. Divide the salad among 4 large chilled serving plates. Top each salad with a sliced avocado half. If serving the salads with chicken, slice each breast diagonally into ½-inch pieces, then transfer one breast to each of the salads. Serve immediately.

thai crunch salad

Makes 4 entrées

We really wanted to re-experience the taste of one of our most popular original pizzas, the Thai Chicken Pizza, but with some added crunch and in a new format: a salad. After some experimentation, we found the perfect combination of crisp wontons, crisp rice sticks, and peanuts, as well as our Thai Peanut Dressing. This is also the first salad that included edamame, now a very popular ingredient. Caution: this salad may be habit forming!

SHOPPING/PANTRY/REFRIGERATOR LIST	HOW MUCH YOU'LL NEED
• Napa cabbage	1 head, cut into $1/4$-inch strips
• Red cabbage	1 small head, cored and chopped
• Carrots	2 large, peeled and julienned
• Scallions (green onions)	2 bunches, thinly sliced (white and pale green parts only)
• English (hothouse) cucumber	1 large, peeled, cored, and julienned
• Cilantro	1 large bunch, chopped
• Cooked shelled edamame (soybeans)	2 cups
• Roasted peanuts	2 cups
• Grilled Garlic Chicken (page 22)	4 breasts
• Lime-Cilantro Dressing (recipe follows)	1 cup
• Fried Wonton Strips (page 118)	4 cups
• Crisp Rice Sticks (page 118)	2 cups
• Ripe Hass avocados (optional)	2, peeled, pitted, cut into $1/2$-inch dice
• Thai Peanut Dressing (recipe follows)	$1/2$ cup

SPECIAL EQUIPMENT
Squeeze bottle or syrup dispenser

PREPARATION

1 Place the cabbages, carrots, scallions, cucumber, cilantro, edamame, and peanuts in a very large mixing bowl and toss to mix.

2 Cut the chicken into $1/2$-inch cubes and add to the mixing bowl.

3 Pour the Lime-Cilantro Dressing into the bowl and toss to mix thoroughly. Gently toss in the Fried Wonton Strips. Divide the salad among 4 very large, chilled serving plates and top with Crisp Rice Sticks.

4 Sprinkle Crisp Rice Sticks over the top of each salad, then use a squeeze bottle or syrup dispenser to drizzle Thai Peanut Dressing over the rice sticks.

5 If serving the salads with avocado, distribute over the salads. Serve immediately.

LIME-CILANTRO DRESSING

Makes 1 cup

SHOPPING/PANTRY/REFRIGERATOR LIST
- Red bell pepper
- Cilantro leaves
- Honey
- White vinegar
- Lime juice
- Light corn syrup
- Dijon mustard
- Asian sesame oil
- Fresh ginger
- Kosher salt
- Ground black pepper
- Extra-virgin olive oil

HOW MUCH YOU'LL NEED
$1/4$ small, cored and cut into $1/2$-inch pieces
1 small bunch, coarsely chopped
1 tablespoon + 2 teaspoons
1 tablespoon + 2 teaspoons
1 tablespoon + $1/2$ teaspoons
$1/2$ teaspoons
2 teaspoons
$1/2$ teaspoon
$1/4$ teaspoon minced
$1/2$ teaspoon
$1/4$ teaspoon
$1/2$ cup

PREPARATION

1 Place the bell pepper and cilantro leaves in the work bowl of a food processor, then add the remaining ingredients except for the olive oil. Process until smooth, 30 to 60 seconds.

2 With the food processor on, add the olive oil in a thin stream and continue processing for 1 minute after all the oil has been added; there should be no oil on the surface. Store covered in the refrigerator for up to 1 week (whisk before using).

THAI PEANUT DRESSING

Makes $1/2$ cup

SHOPPING/PANTRY/REFRIGERATOR LIST
- Creamy peanut butter
- Seasoned rice vinegar
- Honey
- Water
- Soy sauce
- Sugar
- Kosher salt
- Cayenne pepper
- Crushed red pepper flakes
- Canola oil

HOW MUCH YOU'LL NEED
2 tablespoons
1 tablespoon
1 tablespoon
$1^1/_2$ teaspoons
$1^1/_2$ teaspoons
1 tablespoon
$3/_4$ teaspoon
$1/_4$ teaspoon (scant)
Pinch
1 tablespoon

PREPARATION

Whisk together the peanut butter, vinegar, honey, water, and soy sauce. Stir in the sugar, salt, cayenne, and red pepper flakes. Add the oil and continue whisking until smooth. Use immediately or refrigerate for up to 5 days. Bring to room temperature and whisk before using.

waldorf chicken salad

Makes 4 entrées

This is our modern take on an old American favorite. Normally prepared with a heavy cream dressing, we decided to see how the popular ingredients (apple, candied walnuts, etc.) would stand up to a lighter dressing. Served with a light Dijon balsamic vinaigrette, it's become a CPK favorite.

SHOPPING/PANTRY/REFRIGERATOR LIST	HOW MUCH YOU'LL NEED
• Baby field greens	1 pound
• Tart green apples (Granny Smith or Pippin)	2 large or 3 small, cored and thinly sliced
• Celery	3 ribs, sliced diagonally
• Red seedless grapes, halved	1 pound
• Crumbled Gorgonzola cheese	$1/2$ pound
• Grilled Garlic Chicken (page 22)	4 breasts, cut into $1/2$-inch strips
• Candied Walnuts (page 117)	2 cups
• Balsamic vinaigrette or blue cheese dressing	$1/2$ to 1 cup

PREPARATION

Toss all the ingredients with the dressing of your choice in a large mixing bowl. Mix well. Divide among 4 chilled serving plates and serve immediately.

grilled chicken pesto panini

Makes 2 sandwiches

Pesto is a traditional flavor that has never lost its popularity, and we don't think it ever will. We love it! We've blended it with mayo, Larry's all-time favorite condiment, and created a creamy spread—a pesto aioli. It's been our most popular panini sandwich since.

SHOPPING/PANTRY/REFRIGERATOR LIST	HOW MUCH YOU'LL NEED
• Crusty Italian bread	4 $\frac{1}{2}$-inch-thick slices
• Mayonnaise	2 tablespoons
• Fresh basil	1 medium leaf, finely chopped
• Garlic	1 small clove, finely minced
• Sun-dried tomatoes in olive oil	4 halves or 4 tablespoons julienne strips
• Grilled Garlic Chicken (page 22)	1 breast
• Monterey Jack cheese	4 one-ounce slices

SPECIAL EQUIPMENT
Panini grill

PREPARATION

1 Heat an electric panini grill. Coat one side of each slice of bread with nonstick cooking spray and place the bread on a cutting board with the sprayed sides down. Combine the mayonnaise, basil, and garlic, and spread evenly over 2 slices of bread. Drain the sun-dried tomatoes and cut the halves into julienne strips. Distribute the tomato strips over the bread.

2 Slice the chicken with your knife at a 45° angle to the cutting board. Microwave the chicken for 20 seconds so that the entire panini will be warm when served. Lay the chicken slices over the tomato, then top with the cheese slices. Cover with the remaining bread, sprayed side up.

3 Grill according to the instructions that came with your panini grill. When finished, slice each panini in half and serve.

honey-dijon chicken and bacon panini

Makes 2 sandwiches

Larry's grandson, Alex, always ordered his sandwiches with honey-Dijon sauce whenever he visited a CPK, so we decided to give it a permanent place on one of our panini. We added bacon, which complements the sauce perfectly, and we love it—so does Alex.

SHOPPING/PANTRY/REFRIGERATOR LIST	HOW MUCH YOU'LL NEED
• Crusty Italian bread	4 $\frac{1}{2}$-inch-thick slices
• Mayonnaise	2 tablespoons
• Dijon mustard	1 tablespoon
• Clover honey	1$\frac{1}{2}$ teaspoons
• Grilled Garlic Chicken (page 22)	1 breast
• Bacon	4 strips, cooked until crisp
• Monterey Jack cheese	4 one-ounce slices

SPECIAL EQUIPMENT
Panini grill

PREPARATION

1 Heat an electric panini grill. Coat one side of each slice of bread with nonstick cooking spray, and place the slices on a cutting board with the sprayed side down. Combine the mayonnaise, mustard, and honey, and whisk until smooth. Spread evenly over 2 slices of bread.

2 Slice the chicken with your knife at a 45° angle to the cutting board. Microwave the chicken for 20 seconds, so that the entire panini will be warm when served. Lay the chicken slices on the bread, then the bacon over the chicken. Top with sliced cheese. Cover with the remaining bread, sprayed side up.

3 Grill according to the instructions that came with your panini grill. When finished, slice each panini in half and serve.

turkey club panini

Makes 2 sandwiches

This is the perfect example of taking a classic sandwich and kicking it up a notch. We took our Turkey Club Sandwich from our CPK ASAP Restaurants and decided to roll it out as a panini. Now our guests can choose to have an American favorite two different ways.

SHOPPING/PANTRY/REFRIGERATOR LIST	HOW MUCH YOU'LL NEED
• Crusty Italian bread	4 $\frac{1}{2}$-inch-thick slices
• Mayonnaise	1 tablespoon
• Dijon mustard	1 tablespoon
• Hass avocado	$\frac{1}{2}$, sliced
• Roast turkey breast	$\frac{1}{2}$ pound, sliced
• Bacon	4 strips, cooked until crisp
• Roma tomato	1 large
• Monterey Jack cheese	4 one-ounce slices

SPECIAL EQUIPMENT
Panini grill

PREPARATION

1 Heat an electric panini grill. Coat one side of each slice of bread with nonstick cooking spray, and place the bread on a cutting board with the sprayed sides down. Combine the mayonnaise and mustard, and spread evenly over 2 slices of bread. Cover the bread evenly with avocado slices.

2 Meanwhile, microwave the turkey for 20 to 30 seconds, so that the panini will be hot when served. Distribute the turkey, then the bacon, over the avocado. Cut the tomato into ¼-inch slices, and distribute over the bacon. Top with the cheese slices. Cover with the remaining bread, sprayed side up.

3 Grill according to the instructions that came with your panini grill. When finished, slice each panini in half and serve.

vegetarian panini

Makes 2 sandwiches

This wonderful combination of flavors and textures is a favorite among vegetarians and meat-eaters alike.

SHOPPING/PANTRY/REFRIGERATOR LIST	HOW MUCH YOU'LL NEED
• Olive oil	2 teaspoons
• Portobello mushroom	1 large
• Kosher salt	$1/4$ teaspoon
• Ground black pepper	$1/4$ teaspoon
• Red bell pepper	$1/2$ small
• Yellow bell pepper	$1/2$ small
• Sun-dried tomatoes in olive oil	1 tablespoon, mashed
• Fresh basil leaves	1 tablespoon, finely chopped
• Garlic	1 teaspoon, finely chopped
• Mayonnaise	3 tablespoons
• Crusty Italian bread	4 $1/2$-inch-thick slices
• Roma tomato	1 large
• Arugula leaves	1 ounce (1 cup, packed)
• Monterey Jack cheese	4 one-ounce slices

SPECIAL EQUIPMENT
Panini grill

PREPARATION

1 Heat 1 teaspoon of the olive oil in a large frying pan. Cut off the portobello stem even with the cap. Remove any dirt from the mushroom cap. Cut into $1/4$-inch slices. Add to the pan and sprinkle with salt and pepper. Cook until the mushroom edges are lightly browned and the mushroom is cooked, 5 to 6 minutes. Drain in a strainer or colander and keep warm on a foil-covered plate.

2 Reheat the pan with the remaining teaspoon oil. Cut the bell pepper halves into $1/4$-inch × 2-inch strips. Remove any light-colored membrane from the inside. Add to the pan with a sprinkling of salt and pepper. Cook until the peppers are limp, 3 to 4 minutes. Continue cooking over high heat, without stirring, until the pepper strips are slightly charred. Remove with tongs to a plate.

3 Heat an electric panini grill. Coat one side of each slice of bread with nonstick cooking spray and place the bread on a cutting board with the sprayed sides down. Stir together the sun-dried tomato, basil, garlic, and mayonnaise, and spread this mixture evenly on each slice of bread.

4 Distribute the pepper strips over 2 slices of bread and cover those with an even layer of portobello slices. Cut the tomato into ¼-inch slices and distribute over the mushroom slices.

5 Cover the tomato slices with arugula leaves, and finish each panini with a cheese slice. Cover with the remaining bread, sprayed side up.

6 Grill according to the instructions that came with your panini grill. When finished, slice each panini in half and serve.

specialties from our menu

There are certain dishes that the whole family loves to eat. Here is a sampling of those dishes that are also simple and fun to make at home.

curly mac & cheese

Makes 4 to 6 entrées

Judging from the number of adults who order this classic, we know that it is everyone's favorite comfort food.

SHOPPING/PANTRY/REFRIGERATOR LIST
- Kosher salt
- Fusilli
- Heavy cream
- Velveeta

HOW MUCH YOU'LL NEED
1 tablespoon + 2 teaspoons
1½ pounds
1 quart
2 pounds, cubed

PREPARATION

1 Bring 6 quarts of water to a boil with 1 tablespoon of salt. Cook the fusilli until al dente, about 8 minutes. Drain thoroughly.

2 Meanwhile, pour the cream into a large pot. Add the Velveeta and the remaining 2 teaspoons salt, and heat over medium heat, stirring occasionally, until the Velveeta begins to melt.

3 Add the drained pasta and stir well. Continue cooking and stirring occasionally until the Velveeta is completely melted and the sauce begins to thicken, 3 to 4 minutes.

4 Serve in warm bowls.

chicken milanese

Makes 4 entrées

Don't avoid making this delicious dish just because it is breaded and fried. When done correctly, the breading is thin and delicate, and not at all greasy. It's the perfect way to satisfy that craving for fried chicken.

SHOPPING/PANTRY/REFRIGERATOR LIST
- Boneless, skinless chicken breasts
- Egg
- Dry bread crumbs (plain)
- Kosher salt
- Ground white pepper
- Olive oil
- Baby arugula
- Extra-virgin olive oil
- Parmesan cheese
- Checca (recipe follows)
- Lemons

HOW MUCH YOU'LL NEED
8 breasts, 3 to 4 ounces each
1 large
1 cup
1 teaspoon
½ teaspoon
¾ cup
8 cups loosely packed (2 bags)
1 tablespoon
2 ounces, shaved
2 cups
2, cut in half and wrapped in cheesecloth

SPECIAL EQUIPMENT
Meat mallet

PREPARATION

1 Place the chicken breasts between sheets of waxed or parchment paper and pound them to a thickness of ¼ to ⅜ inch. You can also ask your butcher to do this for you.

2 Crack the egg into a shallow bowl or pie plate and beat it lightly with a fork or a whisk. Combine the bread crumbs, salt, and pepper in another shallow bowl or pie plate. Dip both sides of each chicken breast in the egg, shake off excess, and then dip into the breading mixture, coating evenly. Stack the breaded chicken pieces on a plate.

3 Heat half the olive oil in a large sauté pan over medium-high heat. Cook half the chicken breasts on one side until golden brown, about 1½ minutes. Turn and cook the other side for about 1 minute. Remove the chicken to a large serving platter covered with several layers of paper towel. Repeat with the remaining chicken, using remaining olive oil.

4 Using tongs, layer the chicken breasts in the center of 4 large, heated plates or a large serving platter. Distribute the arugula over the chicken and drizzle with the extra-virgin olive oil. Spoon the Checca over the arugula, sprinkle with Parmesan shavings, and serve immediately with lemon halves on the side.

CHECCA

Makes 2 cups

SHOPPING/PANTRY/REFRIGERATOR LIST

- Roma tomatoes
- Garlic
- Kosher salt
- Fresh basil
- Extra-virgin olive oil

HOW MUCH YOU'LL NEED

$3/4$ pound (3 large or 4 small)
$1^1/_2$ teaspoons minced
$3/4$ teaspoon
2 large leaves, finely chopped
$1/4$ cup

PREPARATION

Cut the tops off the tomatoes, and cut then into quarters lengthwise. Remove the seeds, then cut away the inner membranes. Cut the quarters into 2 strips each, then cut those into $1/2$-inch pieces. Place the tomatoes in a mixing bowl and mix in the remaining ingredients. Cover and refrigerate for at least half an hour or up to 24 hours before serving. Stir again and drain any remaining liquid before using.

chicken marsala with linguini

Makes 4 entrées

This dish is an old-time family—and family restaurant—favorite. While it is tradition-
ally made with veal, CPK has updated it using chicken. The dish, and the two that
follow, have been a big part of CPK's evolution, as they represented our first move
into offering full entrées and helped put us on the map as a great spot for dinner.

SHOPPING/PANTRY/REFRIGERATOR LIST	HOW MUCH YOU'LL NEED
• Boneless, skinless chicken breasts	8 breasts, 3 to 4 ounces each
• All-purpose flour	$^3/_4$ cup
• Seasoned salt	2 teaspoons
• Ground white pepper	$^1/_2$ teaspoon
• Dried crushed basil leaves	$^1/_4$ teaspoon
• Olive oil	$^1/_2$ cup
• Dry Marsala wine	$^1/_2$ cup
• Marsala Sauce (recipe follows)	3 cups
• Kosher salt	1 teaspoon
• Ground black pepper	1 teaspoon
• Unsalted butter	4 tablespoons ($^1/_2$ stick)
• Sautéed White Mushrooms (page 122)	10 ounces (about 1$^1/_2$ cups)
• Grilled asparagus (page 120)	5 ounces (1 bundle before cooking)
• Linguini fini (thin linguini)	1 to 1$^1/_2$ pounds, cooked until al dente

SPECIAL EQUIPMENT
Meat mallet

PREPARATION

1 Place the chicken breasts between sheets of waxed or parchment paper and pound them to a thickness of $^1/_4$ to $^3/_8$ inch. You can also ask your butcher to do this for you.

2 Combine the flour, seasoned salt, white pepper, and basil in a pie plate. Coat each chicken breast with this mixture and shake off any excess. Lay the chicken pieces in a dish (they may be stacked).

3 Heat half the oil in a large frying pan over medium-high heat. Cook half of the chicken breasts in the hot oil on one side until golden brown, about 1$^1/_2$ minutes. Carefully turn them and cook on the other side for about 20 seconds more. Remove the chicken to a platter, heat the remaining oil, and repeat with the remaining chicken. Cover the cooked chicken with foil to keep it warm.

4 Remove the pan from the heat and add the Marsala wine. Place back on the heat and cook for about 30 seconds, being careful not to allow the wine to catch fire. Add the sauce to the pan and the salt and black pepper. Add the butter and then the Sautéed Mushrooms and grilled asparagus, and cook over medium heat, stirring, for about 1½ minutes.

5 Add the linguini to the sauce and toss to coat well. Layer the chicken pieces to one side of heated serving plates, large pasta bowls, or a large serving platter. Using tongs, mound the pasta next to the chicken. Pour any remaining sauce, mushrooms, and asparagus over the chicken and pasta, and serve immediately.

MARSALA SAUCE

Makes 3 cups

SHOPPING/PANTRY/REFRIGERATOR LIST

- Olive oil (not extra virgin)
- Shallots
- Garlic
- Dry Marsala wine
- Chicken stock
- Chicken bouillon cube

HOW MUCH YOU'LL NEED

1 tablespoon
2 tablespoons finely chopped
1 tablespoon finely chopped
1 cup
2 cups
1

PREPARATION

1 Heat a heavy 2-quart saucepan over medium heat. Add the oil and then the shallots and garlic, and cook, stirring constantly, until they just begin to brown, 1 to 2 minutes; do not let them burn or they will give your sauce a very bitter flavor. Stir in the Marsala and cook for 1 minute.

2 Add the chicken stock and bouillon cube, bring to a boil, and reduce the heat so that the sauce simmers. Continue cooking for 10 minutes to reduce slightly. Remove from the heat and pour the sauce through a mesh strainer. (It is all right if some of the shallot and garlic pieces pass through the strainer.) Use immediately or cool and store covered in the refrigerator for up to 3 days.

chicken piccata with spaghettini

Makes 4 entrées

Any dish called "piccata" always has two elements: lemon and capers. The tanginess of these two ingredients complements the richness of the olive oil, making for a light, well-balanced dish.

SHOPPING/PANTRY/REFRIGERATOR LIST	HOW MUCH YOU'LL NEED
• Boneless, skinless chicken breasts	8 breasts, 3 to 4 ounces each
• All-purpose flour	$3/4$ cup
• Seasoned salt	2 teaspoons
• Crushed dried basil leaves	$1/4$ teaspoon
• Ground white pepper	$1/2$ teaspoon
• Olive oil	$1/2$ cup
• Piccata Cream Sauce (recipe follows)	3 cups
• Kosher salt	2 teaspoons
• Ground black pepper	1 teaspoon
• Unsalted butter	4 tablespoons ($1/2$ stick)
• Capers	6 tablespoons, drained
• Italian (flat-leaf) parsley	2 tablespoons, chopped
• Spaghettini	1 to $1 1/2$ pounds, cooked until al dente
• Lemon	1, sliced $1/4$-inch thick into 8 slices
• Italian parsley	4 large sprigs for garnish

SPECIAL EQUIPMENT
Meat mallet

PREPARATION

1 Place the chicken breasts between sheets of waxed or parchment paper and pound them to a thickness of $1/4$ to $3/8$ inch. You can also ask your butcher to do this for you.

2 Combine the flour, seasoned salt, basil, and white pepper in a pie plate. Coat each chicken breast with this mixture and shake off any excess.

Lay the chicken pieces on another dish (they may be stacked).

3 Heat half the oil in a large frying pan over medium-high heat. Cook half the chicken breasts in the hot oil on one side until golden brown, about $1 1/2$ minutes. Carefully turn the chicken and cook on the other side for about 20 seconds. Remove the first half of the chicken pieces to a platter. Heat the remaining oil and repeat with the remaining chicken. Cover the cooked chicken with foil to keep it warm.

4 Add the Piccata Cream Sauce to the pan along with the salt and black pepper. Add the butter, capers, and parsley and cook over medium heat, stirring, for about 1½ minutes. Add the pasta and lemon slices to the sauce and toss to coat well.

5 Layer the chicken pieces to one side of 4 heated serving plates, large pasta bowls, or a large serving platter. Using tongs, mound the pasta next to the chicken. Pour any remaining sauce over the chicken and pasta, garnish with parsley sprigs, and serve immediately.

PICCATA CREAM SAUCE

Makes 3 cups

SHOPPING/PANTRY/REFRIGERATOR LIST
- Olive oil (not extra-virgin)
- Shallots
- Garlic
- Dry white wine (such as Chablis)
- Chicken stock
- Fresh lemon juice
- Kosher salt
- Heavy cream

HOW MUCH YOU'LL NEED
1 tablespoon + 1½ teaspoons
6 tablespoons, finely chopped
1 tablespoon + 1½ teaspoons, finely chopped
¾ cup
2 cups
½ cup
1 tablespoon
1 cup

PREPARATION

1 Heat a heavy nonreactive saucepan over medium heat. Add the oil and heat it through. Add the shallots and garlic, and cook, stirring constantly to prevent them from burning, for about 3 minutes. Stir in the wine and simmer for 5 minutes. Stir in the stock, lemon juice, and salt and bring to a boil. Lower the heat and simmer for 10 minutes.

2 Pour the sauce through a fine-mesh strainer. Use immediately, or cool and refrigerate for up to 3 days. Just before using the sauce, add the cream, whisking thoroughly.

the greek pizza

Makes one 13-inch pizza or two 9-inch pizzas

CPK has had tremendous success with salad pizzas, and we're constantly look-
ing for more that will make sense. That is how we came to this pizza. It combines
all of the elements of a traditional Greek salad: creamy feta, sweet red onions,
cucumbers, and a tangy lemon-herb vinaigrette. Just hold the lettuce and eat
with your hands. What could be better? Serving the Tzatziki Sauce on the side
provides the perfect excuse for dipping your pizza.

SHOPPING/PANTRY/REFRIGERATOR LIST	HOW MUCH YOU'LL NEED
• Traditional Pizza Dough (page 14)	1 pound
• Extra-virgin olive oil	2 tablespoons
• Mozzarella cheese	6 ounces, grated (2 cups)
• Grilled Greek Chicken (page 22)	2 breasts, cut into $1/2$-inch pieces
• Greek Salad (page 119)	3 cups
• Tzatziki Sauce (recipe follows)	$3/4$ cup
• Feta cheese	1 ounce (about $1/4$ cup), crumbled
• Fresh Italian (flat-leaf) parsley	2 teaspoons chopped

SPECIAL EQUIPMENT
1-inch pastry brush, 16-inch pizza stone,
wooden pizza peel, squeeze bottle or
syrup dispenser

PREPARATION

1 Place a seasoned (or oiled) pizza stone in the
middle of the oven and preheat to 450° F, at
least 30 minutes.

2 Roll and spread the dough into one 13-inch
or two 9-inch circles and place on a floured
pizza peel (see page 18 for instructions on handling and shaping pizza dough). If you are more
comfortable working with one piece of dough at a
time, you can shape and dress the second piece
while the first is in the oven. If making 2 pizzas,
split all the topping measurements in half.

3 Brush the dough with olive oil to within an
inch of the edge, and spread the grated mozzarella to within $1/2$ inch of the outer edge.
Distribute the chicken over the cheese.

4 Transfer the pizza(s) to the oven and bake for 8
to 10 minutes, or until the crust is golden
brown and the cheese at the center is melted and
bubbly.

5 Meanwhile, prepare the Greek Salad and
Tzatziki Sauce. Place the sauce in a squeeze
bottle or syrup dispenser.

6 Use the peel to remove the pizza(s) from the oven. Slice as desired. Spoon the dressed salad over the pizza(s). Sprinkle with feta cheese, then drizzle with half the Tzatziki Sauce. Sprinkle with chopped parsley. Serve immediately, with the remaining sauce on the side.

TZATZIKI SAUCE

Makes $3/4$ cup

SHOPPING/PANTRY/REFRIGERATOR LIST
- Mayonnaise
- Plain yogurt
- Sour cream
- Feta cheese
- Cucumber
- Dried mint leaves

HOW MUCH YOU'LL NEED
$1/4$ cup
3 tablespoons
3 tablespoons
1 ounce
$1 1/2$ tablespoons, peeled, seeded, and diced
$1/2$ teaspoon

SPECIAL EQUIPMENT
Blender or small food processor

PREPARATION
Place all the ingredients in a blender or small food processor and process until smooth. This sauce will keep for up to 5 days in the refrigerator. Whisk before using.

jamaican jerk chicken pizza

Makes one 13-inch pizza or two 9-inch pizzas

The complex flavors of a traditional Jamaican jerk seasoning are sweet, hot, and tangy all at once. This seasoning lends itself perfectly to pizza, both as a rub for the chicken and as a seasoning for the sauce. If you're trying to identify that unusual flavor in the blend, it's probably allspice, which is absolutely indispensable. Too hot for your family? Cool it down with a yogurt- or fruit-based drink. Have a great day, mon!

SHOPPING/PANTRY/REFRIGERATOR LIST	HOW MUCH YOU'LL NEED
• Traditional or Honey-Wheat Pizza Dough (pages 14, 17)	1 pound
• Caribbean Sauce (recipe follows)	Scant 1/2 cup
• Mozzarella cheese	7 ounces, grated (2 1/3 cup)
• Roasted red and yellow peppers (page 120)	1 of each color
• Onion	1/2 small, thinly sliced
• Bacon (optional)	2 strips, cooked and chopped
• Grilled Jamaican Jerk Chicken (page 22)	2 breasts, cut into 1/2-inch pieces
• Scallions (green onions)	2, thinly sliced (white and pale green parts only)

SPECIAL EQUIPMENT
16-inch pizza stone, wooden pizza peel

PREPARATION

1 Place a seasoned (or oiled) pizza stone in the middle of the oven and preheat to 450° F, at least 30 minutes.

2 Roll and shape the dough into one 13-inch or two 9-inch circles and place on a floured pizza peel (see page 18 for instructions on handling and shaping pizza dough). If you are more comfortable working with one piece of dough at a time, you can shape and dress the second piece while the first is in the oven. If making 2 pizzas, split all the topping ingredients in half.

3 Spread the cooled Caribbean Sauce to within 1 inch of the outer edge of the dough. Set aside 1/3 cup of mozzarella and sprinkle the rest to within 1/2 inch of the edge of the dough. Distribute the pepper pieces over the cheese. Separate the onion rings and place them over the peppers, followed by the bacon (if desired) and chicken. Sprinkle the remaining mozzarella over the pizza.

4 Transfer the pizza to the oven and bake for 8 to 10 minutes, or until the crust is golden brown and the cheese at the center is melted and bubbly. Slice. Garnish with scallions and serve.

CARIBBEAN SAUCE

Makes a scant $\frac{1}{2}$ cup

Start with your favorite bottled Thai-style sweet-hot chili sauce, available in the Asian section of better supermarkets, and give it a Caribbean twist with jerk seasoning.

SHOPPING/PANTRY/REFRIGERATOR LIST
- Wondra (quick-dissolving) flour
- Sweet chili sauce
- Jamaican jerk seasoning (see page 000)

HOW MUCH YOU'LL NEED
1 teaspoon
$\frac{1}{3}$ cup
$\frac{1}{2}$ teaspoon

PREPARATION

1 In a small mixing bowl, whisk the flour with 1 teaspoon cold water, breaking up any clumps. Whisk in the chili sauce, followed by the seasoning blend, and mix well.

2 Pour the mixture into a small pot and cook over high heat, stirring constantly, until thickened, 3 to 4 minutes. Transfer to a bowl and cool completely before using.

vegetarian pizza with japanese eggplant and goat cheese

Makes one 13-inch pizza or two 9-inch pizzas

Veggie pizzas take all sorts of toppings, and CPK's have certainly evolved over the years. This pizza is extremely satisfying because of the "meatiness" of the grilled eggplant and the tartness of the goat cheese.

SHOPPING/PANTRY/REFRIGERATOR LIST	HOW MUCH YOU'LL NEED
• Baby broccoli (broccolini)	1 bunch
• Frozen corn kernels	$\frac{1}{2}$ cup, thawed
• Kosher salt	Pinch
• Ground black pepper	Pinch
• Red onion	$\frac{1}{2}$ small, thinly sliced
• Sun-dried tomatoes in olive oil	4 halves or 4 tablespoons julienne strips
• Traditional or Honey-Wheat Pizza Dough (pages 14, 17)	1 pound
• Marinara/Pizza Sauce (page 21)	6 tablespoons
• Mozzarella cheese	7 ounces, grated ($2\frac{1}{3}$ cups)
• Grilled Japanese eggplant (page 120)	2 eggplants, cut per the recipe
• Sautéed White Mushrooms (page 122)	$\frac{1}{2}$ cup
• Goat cheese (chevre; optional)	2 ounces

SPECIAL EQUIPMENT
16-inch pizza stone, wooden pizza peel

PREPARATION

1 Place a seasoned (or oiled) pizza stone in the middle of the oven and preheat to 450° F, at least 30 minutes.

2 Cut away the bottom of each broccoli stem at an angle. Starting from that point, cut the stems into 1½-inch pieces, always maintaining the same angle, stopping 2 to 3 inches from the tops.

3 Blanch the broccolini in rapidly boiling water for about 1 minute. Using a wire skimmer, remove the broccolini and immediately plunge it into an ice-water bath to stop the cooking and retain the bright green color. Once the broccolini is cool, drain and pat dry.

4 Heat a small, heavy frying pan over high heat. Place the corn kernels in the pan and roast them, stirring often, for about 10 minutes. Remove from the heat and sprinkle with salt and pepper.

5 Separate the rings of the onion. Drain the tomatoes well and cut halves into julienne strips.

6 Roll and shape the dough into one 13-inch or two 9-inch circles and place on a floured pizza peel (see page 18 for instructions on handling and shaping pizza dough). If you are more comfortable working with one piece of dough at a time, you can shape and dress the second piece while the first is in the oven. If making 2 pizzas, split all the toppings in half.

7 Spread the sauce to within 1 inch of the outer edge of the dough. Reserve ⅓ cup of the moz-zarella and distribute the rest over the sauce, reserving a small amount, to within ½ inch of the outer edge of the dough. Spread the eggplant over the cheese, followed by the mushrooms, onion rings, and sun-dried tomatoes. Sprinkle the corn over the other vegetables and top with the broccoli.

8 Sprinkle the remaining mozzarella over the pizza. If using goat cheese, break it into small pieces and distribute over the pizza.

9 Transfer the pizza to the oven and bake for 8 to 10 minutes, or until the crust is golden brown and the cheese at the center is melted and bubbly. Slice and serve.

sicilian pizza

Makes one 14-inch pizza or two 10-inch pizzas

This is one of our favorites. We wanted to create a true meat lover's pizza, but with more interesting Italian meats—some you wouldn't necessarily find in other restaurants. When we paired the capocollo ham with a new spicy tomato sauce, we knew we had a hit. But what really makes this pizza is its thin crust; we introduced Neapolitan pizza crusts in our restaurant with this pizza.

SHOPPING/PANTRY/REFRIGERATOR LIST	HOW MUCH YOU'LL NEED
• Neapolitan Pizza Dough (page 16)	14 ounces
• Spicy Marinara Sauce (page 21)	1/4 cup
• Fontina cheese	2 1/2 ounces, grated (2/3 cup)
• Mozzarella cheese	3 ounces, grated (1 cup)
• Italian sausage	6 ounces, cooked and crumbled
• Capocollo ham	12 slices
• Italian salami	2 ounces, sliced
• Parmesan cheese	2 ounces, shaved (1/2 cup)
• Dried oregano leaves	2 teaspoons
• Fresh basil leaves	4 large, julienned

SPECIAL EQUIPMENT
16-inch pizza stone, wooden pizza peel

PREPARATION

1 Place a seasoned (or oiled) pizza stone in the middle of the oven and preheat to 450° F, at least 30 minutes.

2 Roll and shape the dough into one 14-inch or two 10-inch circles and place on a floured pizza peel (see page 16 for instructions on handling and shaping pizza dough). If making 2 pizzas, work with only 1 piece of dough at a time, as your pizza stone may not accommodate more.

3 Spread the sauce over the surface of the dough and sprinkle the grated cheeses over the sauce. Distribute the crumbled sausage over the cheeses and top with the sliced ham. Cut the salami slices into 1/8-inch julienne, and distribute over the ham. Top evenly with the Parmesan shavings and sprinkle with the oregano.

4 Transfer the pizza to the oven and bake for 5 to 8 minutes, or until the crust is golden brown and the cheese at the center is melted and bubbly. If preparing another pizza, do so while the first is in the oven. Slice, garnish with basil, and serve.

white pizza with bacon

Makes one 13-inch pizza or two 9-inch pizzas

We tried several variations of *pizza bianca*, but fell in love with this blended cheese recipe. The spinach adds a touch of color and a CPK twist to this "white" pizza.

SHOPPING/PANTRY/REFRIGERATOR LIST	HOW MUCH YOU'LL NEED
• Olive oil	1 teaspoon
• Minced garlic	2 teaspoons
• Fresh spinach	4 cups or $2/3$ of a 6-ounce bag
• Kosher salt	Pinch
• Ground black pepper	Pinch
• Traditional Pizza Dough (page 14)	1 pound
• Mozzarella cheese	3 ounces, grated (1 cup)
• Bacon (optional)	2 slices, cooked and chopped ($1/4$ cup)
• Fontina cheese	$2^{1}/2$ ounces, grated ($2/3$ cup)
• Parmesan cheese	1 ounce, grated (2 tablespoons)
• Romano cheese	1 ounce, grated (2 tablespoons)
• Ricotta cheese	3 ounces ($1/2$ cup)

SPECIAL EQUIPMENT
16-inch pizza stone, wooden pizza peel

PREPARATION

1 Place a seasoned (or oiled) pizza stone in the middle of the oven and preheat to 450° F, at least 30 minutes.

2 Heat the oil in a large frying pan. Add the garlic and cook, stirring constantly, for about 1 minute or until garlic just begins to brown. Place the spinach, salt, and pepper in the pan and cook, stirring, until the leaves are just wilted, about 1 minute. Drain and immediately spread the spinach on a plate to cool to room temperature.

3 Roll and shape the dough into one 13-inch or two 9-inch circles and place on a floured pizza peel (see page 18 for instructions on handling and shaping pizza dough). If you are more comfortable working with one piece of dough at a time, you can shape and dress the second piece while the first is in the oven. If making 2 pizzas, split all the topping ingredients in half.

4 Spread the cooled spinach over the dough to within 1 inch of the outer edge. Top that with the mozzarella and bacon, if desired. Distribute the remaining cheeses over the mozzarella, finishing with dollops of ricotta.

5 Transfer the pizza to the oven and bake for 8 to 10 minutes, or until the crust is golden brown and the cheese at the center is melted and bubbly. Slice and serve.

"the works" pizza

Makes one 13-inch pizza or two 9-inch pizzas

When you reminisce about the pizzas you grew up on—especially the one from the corner pizzeria—your mouth may well start watering. That's what we were hoping for with this pizza! It's pure American 1960s–style—the "gimme-one-with-everything, Gino!"

SHOPPING/PANTRY/REFRIGERATOR LIST	HOW MUCH YOU'LL NEED
• Traditional or Honey-Wheat Pizza Dough (pages 14, 17)	1 pound
• Marinara/Pizza Sauce (page 21)	6 tablespoons
• Mozzarella cheese	7 ounces, grated (2 1/3 cups)
• Italian sausage	6 ounces, cooked and crumbled
• Sautéed White Mushrooms (page 122)	1/2 cup
• Onion	1/2 small, thinly sliced
• Pepperoni slices	32 (about 8 ounces)
• Black olives	1/2 cup sliced
• Green bell pepper	1 small, cut into 1/4-inch rings

SPECIAL EQUIPMENT
16-inch pizza stone, wooden pizza peel

PREPARATION

1 Place a seasoned (or oiled) pizza stone in the middle of your oven and preheat to 450° F, at least 30 minutes.

2 Roll and shape the dough into one 13-inch or two 9-inch circles and place on a floured pizza peel (see page 18 for instructions on handling and shaping pizza dough). If you are more comfortable working with one piece of dough at a time, you can shape and dress the second piece while the first is in the oven. If making 2 pizzas, split all the topping ingredients in half.

3 Spread the sauce to within 1 inch of the outer edge of the dough. Reserve 1/3 cup of mozzarella and distribute the rest over the sauce to within 1/2 inch of the outer edge of the dough.

4 In this order, distribute the topping ingredients over the mozzarella: crumbled sausage, mushrooms, onion, pepperoni, black olives, and bell pepper. Finish by sprinkling the remaining 1/3 cup of mozzarella over the entire pizza.

5 Transfer the pizza to the oven and bake for 10 to 15 minutes, or until the crust is golden brown and the cheese at the center is melted and bubbly. Slice and serve.

chipotle chicken pizza

Makes one 13-inch pizza or two 9-inch pizzas

Chipotle chiles (smoked jalapeños) have become a key ingredient not only in Southwest and Tex-Mex cooking but also in other dishes in the United States. CPK's other Mexican pizzas (Tostada, Southwest Burrito) have always been popular; so we decided to give those traditional flavors a bit of a kick.

SHOPPING/PANTRY/REFRIGERATOR LIST	HOW MUCH YOU'LL NEED
• Anaheim chiles	2
• Chipotle sauce (bottled)	6 tablespoons
• Grilled Garlic Chicken (page 22)	2 breasts, cut into ½-inch cubes
• Traditional or Honey-Wheat Pizza Dough (page 14, 17)	1 pound
• Mozzarella cheese	4 ounces, grated (1⅓ cups)
• Añejo enchilado cheese	2½ ounces, shredded (1 cup)
• Lime Cream Sauce (recipe follows)	6 tablespoons
• Cilantro leaves	2 teaspoons finely chopped
• Chipotle Salsa (recipe follows)	1 cup

SPECIAL EQUIPMENT
16-inch pizza stone, wooden pizza peel, squeeze bottle or syrup dispenser

PREPARATION

1 Place a seasoned (or oiled) pizza stone in the middle of your oven and preheat to 450° F, at least 30 minutes.

2 Cook the chiles over an open flame until the skin is black and blistered. (This can also be done in a very hot, ungreased cast iron pan.) Put the chiles in a small bowl and cover with plastic wrap. Let cool for 10 minutes, then rub the charred skin off with paper towels (do not use water). Remove the stems and seeds, and cut the chiles lengthwise into ¼-inch strips.

3 Toss the chipotle sauce with the chicken pieces in a bowl until coated.

4 Roll and shape the dough into one 13-inch or two 9-inch circles and place on a floured pizza peel (see page 18 for instructions on handling and shaping pizza dough). If you are more comfortable working with one piece of dough at a time, you can shape and dress the second piece while the first is in the oven. If making 2 pizzas, split all the topping ingredients in half.

5 Set aside ⅓ cup of the mozzarella and sprinkle the rest to within ½ inch of the edge of the dough.

6 Distribute the chicken over the mozzarella, cover that with the chile strips, then top with enchilado cheese. Sprinkle the remaining mozzarella over the entire pizza.

7 Transfer the pizza to the oven and bake for 8 to 10 minutes, or until the crust is golden brown and the cheese at the center is melted and bubbly. Slice.

8 Drizzle the Lime Cream Sauce over the pizza and sprinkle with the cilantro. Serve with a mound of Chipotle Salsa in the middle of the pizza.

LIME CREAM SAUCE
Makes about ²/₃ cup

SHOPPING/PANTRY/REFRIGERATOR LIST	HOW MUCH YOU'LL NEED
• Cilantro leaves	1 teaspoon finely chopped
• Shallot	1¹/₂ teaspoons finely minced
• Mayonnaise	¹/₄ cup
• Sour cream	¹/₄ cup
• Lime juice	2 teaspoons
• Sugar	1¹/₂ teaspoons
• Kosher salt	Pinch

PREPARATION
Place all of the ingredients in a blender or small food processor and blend until smooth. Use immediately, or cover and refrigerate for up to 3 days. Stir well before using.

CHIPOTLE SALSA

Makes 1 cup

SHOPPING/PANTRY/REFRIGERATOR LIST

- Frozen corn kernels
- Cooked black beans
- Tomato salsa
- Chipotle sauce

HOW MUCH YOU'LL NEED

$\frac{1}{4}$ cup, thawed
$\frac{1}{4}$ cup, drained and rinsed
$\frac{1}{2}$ cup
2 teaspoons

PREPARATION

1 Heat a heavy frying pan over high heat. Place the corn kernels in the pan and roast them for about 10 minutes, stirring often.

2 Place the corn in a mixing bowl and add the remaining ingredients. Mix well. Use immediately, or cool, cover, and refrigerate for up to 3 days.

cpkids pizza party!

From the day we opened our fist CPK, we've known that kids needed their own menu and should not have to eat off their parents' plates. We are dedicated to giving kids the same variety that our adult menu has. This requires constantly adding new items to liven things up. Here are some of our traditional CPKids! favorites to inspire you and your family to have a pizza party at home. Be sure to try some combinations you've never tried before. That's precisely how we've come up with some of our most popular pizzas.

cpkids' mushroom, pepperoni, and sausage pizza

Makes one 13-inch pizza, two 9-inch pizzas, or four 6-inch pizzas

This is the kid's version of "The Works" Pizza, and was actually around long before CPK introduced the latter. It is a perfect example of how we are inspired by our youngest customers!

SHOPPING/PANTRY/REFRIGERATOR LIST
- Traditional Pizza Dough (page 14)
- Marinara/Pizza Sauce (page 21)
- Mozzarella cheese
- Italian sausage
- Pepperoni slices
- Sautéed White Mushrooms (page 122)

HOW MUCH YOU'LL NEED
1 pound
$\frac{1}{2}$ cup
6 ounces, grated (2 cups)
6 ounces, cooked and crumbled
24 (about 6 ounces)
$\frac{1}{4}$ cup

SPECIAL EQUIPMENT
16-inch pizza stone, wooden pizza peel

PREPARATION

1 Place a seasoned (or oiled) pizza stone in the middle of your oven and preheat to 450° F, at least 30 minutes.

2 Roll and shape the dough into one 13-inch, two 9-inch or four 6-inch circles and place on a floured pizza peel (see page 18 for instructions on handling and shaping pizza dough). If making 6-inch pizzas, prepare 2 at a time.

3 Spread the sauce to within $\frac{1}{2}$ inch of the outer edge of the dough. Distribute the mozzarella over the sauce, then the crumbled sausage over the cheese. Cover those ingredients with sliced pepperoni and mushrooms.

4 Transfer the pizza(s) to the oven and bake for 6 to 10 minutes, or until the crust is golden brown and the cheese at the center is melted and bubbly. Smaller pizzas will bake more quickly. Slice and serve.

VARIATIONS
- **CPKids' Traditional Cheese Pizza:** Prepare the above pizza, omitting the sausage, pepperoni, and mushrooms.
- **CPKids' Pepperoni Pizza:** Prepare the Traditional Cheese Pizza, and top with 24 slices of pepperoni.

create-your-own pizza

Makes two 13-inch pizzas, four 9-inch pizzas, or eight 6-inch pizzas (or as many storebought pizza crusts as you need)

Kids not only love to eat pizza, they love to make it. Here's a recipe that provides both the meal and the entertainment for a kids' party. Have the kids top their individual pizzas or their portions of a larger pizza. Either way, make sure that they work quickly, so that the dough can be moved to the oven.

....

SHOPPING/PANTRY/REFRIGERATOR LIST	HOW MUCH YOU'LL NEED
• Traditional Pizza Dough (page 14)	2 pounds
• Marinara/Pizza Sauce (page 21)	2 cups

TOPPINGS:
- Sliced pepperoni
- Grated mozzarella cheese
- Grated Monterey Jack cheese
- Grated Swiss cheese
- Sautéed White Mushrooms (page 122)
- Sliced black or green olives
- Cocktail wieners or sliced hot dog
- Canned tuna in olive oil
- Chili con carne
- Canned corn, drained
- Sliced deli meats (cut into strips)
- Pineapple chunks, drained
- Cooked hamburger meat, crumbled
- Cooked Italian sausage, crumbled
- Popcorn chicken
- Crumbled bacon

....

SPECIAL EQUIPMENT
16-inch pizza stone, wooden pizza peel

PREPARATION

1 Place a seasoned (or oiled) pizza stone in the middle of your oven and preheat to 450° F for at least 30 minutes.

2 If using homemade dough, either roll and shape it according to the instructions on page 18, or have the kids roll and shape their own. Top the pizzas as desired.

3 Transfer to the pizza stone and bake for 6 to 10 minutes, or until the crusts are browned on the bottom. Remove from the oven, and have each chef claim his or her own.

valentine's day pizza

Makes 1 large, 2 medium, or 4 individual pizzas

Is there anyone who doesn't think of chocolate when they think of Valentine's Day? Here is a warm dessert pizza, suitable for one or two couples, or even a party, that's the perfect prelude to an evening of romance or fun.

SHOPPING/PANTRY/REFRIGERATOR LIST	HOW MUCH YOU'LL NEED
• Traditional or Honey-Wheat Pizza Dough (pages 14, 17) or	1 pound
• Neapolitan Pizza Dough (page 16)	14 ounces
• Confectioners' sugar	1/2 cup
• Frozen raspberries	12-ounce bag, thawed
• Chocolate sauce or syrup	1/2 cup
• Fresh strawberries	1 cup sliced
• Vanilla or chocolate ice cream	As desired
• Whipped cream	No limit

SPECIAL EQUIPMENT
16-inch pizza stone, wooden pizza peel, mesh strainer

PREPARATION

1 Place a seasoned (or oiled) pizza stone in the middle of your oven and preheat to 450° F, at least 30 minutes.

2 Roll and shape the dough into 1 large, 2 medium, or 4 individual heart-shaped crusts and place on a floured pizza peel (see page 18 for instructions on handling and shaping pizza dough). If making 6-inch pizzas, prepare 2 at a time.

3 Place half the sugar in a fine-mesh strainer and cover the dough with a thin, even layer of sugar. This will caramelize as the pizza bakes.

4 Transfer the sugar-covered pizza dough to the oven and bake for 5 to 10 minutes, depending on the thickness of the dough. The crust should be golden brown and thoroughly cooked. Use the peel or 2 broad spatulas to remove the crust(s), and place on individual serving plates or a serving platter.

5 Meanwhile, puree the raspberries in a blender or food processor, then pass through the strainer to remove the seeds. Sweeten with the remaining sugar.

6 Top the crust while still warm with any or all of the following: the pureed raspberries, chocolate sauce, strawberries, ice cream, or whipped cream. Serve immediately after topping.

fourth of july pizza

Makes 1 large pizza

This is formed into a rectangle to resemble Old Glory.

SHOPPING/PANTRY/REFRIGERATOR LIST	HOW MUCH YOU'LL NEED
• Traditional or Honey-Wheat Pizza Dough (pages 14, 17) or	1 pound
• Neapolitan Pizza Dough (page 16)	14 ounces
• Confectioners' sugar	½ cup
• Semi-sweet chocolate chips	1 (12-ounce) bag (2 cups)
• White chocolate chips	1 cup
• Fresh blueberries	2 cups
• Fresh raspberries	4 cups
• Whipped cream	2 to 3 cups
• Vanilla ice cream	As desired

SPECIAL EQUIPMENT
16-inch pizza stone, 12 x 16-inch cookie sheet (rimless), mesh strainer

PREPARATION

1 Place a seasoned (or oiled) pizza stone in the middle of your oven and preheat to 450° F, at least 30 minutes.

2 Spread the dough on a lightly greased cookie sheet. Place half the sugar in a fine-mesh strainer and cover the dough with a thin, even layer of sugar. This will caramelize as the pizza bakes.

3 Transfer the sugar-covered pizza dough to the oven and bake for 5 to 10 minutes, depending on the thickness of the dough. The crust should be golden brown and thoroughly cooked.

4 Remove dough from the oven, spread the semi-sweet chocolate chips evenly over the hot crust, and allow them to melt. Let the crust cool completely and the chocolate harden somewhat.

5 Decorate the pizza with blueberries and white chocolate chip "stars," and with raspberry and whipped cream stripes. Serve with vanilla ice cream.

halloween jack-o-lantern pizza

Makes one large pizza, two medium pizzas, or four individual pizzas

We can't trick you! This is really a pumpkin pie on a pizza crust.

SHOPPING/PANTRY/REFRIGERATOR LIST

- Traditional or Honey-Wheat Pizza Dough (pages 14, 17)
- Confectioners' sugar
- Pumpkin pie filling
- Mini chocolate chips
- Chocolate kisses
- Whipped cream
- Candy corn (chicken's teeth)

HOW MUCH YOU'LL NEED

1 pound

1/4 cup
2 cups canned
1 (12-ounce) bag (2 cups)
2 per pizza
2 cups
1 cup

SPECIAL EQUIPMENT
16-inch pizza stone, wooden pizza peel, mesh strainer

PREPARATION

1 Place a seasoned (or oiled) pizza stone in the middle of your oven and preheat to 450° F for at least 30 minutes.

2 Roll and shape the dough into 1 large, 2 medium, or 4 individual pumpkin-shaped crusts with raised rims, and place on a floured pizza peel (see page 18 for instructions on handling and shaping pizza dough). If making 4 pizzas, prepare 2 at a time.

3 Place the sugar in a fine-mesh strainer and sift a thin, even layer of sugar over the dough. This will caramelize as the pizza bakes.

4 Transfer the pizza to the oven and bake for 5 minutes to set the dough. Once all of the crusts have been partially cooked, spread each with a thin layer of pumpkin pie filling and return to the oven for another 5 to 10 minutes, or until the filling is set. Remove from the oven and allow the pizzas to cool.

5 Decorate the pizzas using mini chocolate chips to represent the vertical lines, whipped cream for the eyes and mouth, chocolate kisses for the eyeballs, and candy corn for the teeth.

thanksgiving sweet potato pizza

Makes one 13-inch pizza or two 9-inch pizzas

If you think that candied yams are a gooey mess to serve, but you still love them, then this pizza is for you!

SHOPPING/PANTRY/REFRIGERATOR LIST
- Sweet potatoes or yams
- Traditional or Honey-Wheat Pizza Dough (pages 14, 17)
- Light brown sugar
- Kosher salt
- Unsalted butter
- Mini marshmallows (optional)

HOW MUCH YOU'LL NEED
2 to 3 (1½ pounds)
1 pound

½ cup packed
½ teaspoon
4 tablespoons (½ stick), cubed
2 cups

SPECIAL EQUIPMENT
16-inch pizza stone, wooden pizza peel

PREPARATION

1 Preheat your oven to 375° F. Wash the sweet potatoes and place them in a glass baking dish. Bake for about 1 hour, or until a knife inserts easily into the thickest part of a potato. Remove the potatoes from the oven and raise the temperature to 450° F. Heat a seasoned pizza stone for at least 30 minutes.

2 Allow the sweet potatoes to cool slightly, then peel them with a paring knife. Slice into ¼-inch rounds and let cool on your cutting board.

3 Roll and shape the dough into one 13-inch or two 9-inch circles and place on a floured pizza peel (see page 000 for instructions on handling and shaping pizza dough). If you are more comfortable working with one piece of dough at a time, you can shape and dress the second piece while the first is in the oven. If making 2 pizzas, split all the topping ingredients in half.

4 Place overlapping rounds of sweet potato over the top of the pizza, leaving a ½-inch border of dough. Sprinkle with an even layer of brown sugar, then with salt. Distribute small cubes of butter evenly over the surface, avoiding the dough border. Cover with marshmallows. (It's all right if there are pieces of sweet potato showing.)

5 Transfer the pizza to the oven and bake for 8 to 12 minutes, or until the crust is golden brown and the marshmallows are melted and well colored. Remove from the oven, slice, and serve.

potato pancake pizza

Makes one 14-inch pizza or two 10-inch pizzas

It's a pizza. It's a latke. It's a pizza and a latke—and this latke has the added advantage of not being fried in oil!

SHOPPING/PANTRY/REFRIGERATOR LIST	HOW MUCH YOU'LL NEED
• Neapolitan Pizza Dough (page 16)	14 ounces
• Russet potatoes	2 large, baked and cooled
• Onion	1 small, finely chopped
• Kosher salt	$\frac{1}{2}$ teaspoon
• Ground black pepper	$\frac{1}{4}$ teaspoon
• Olive oil	1 tablespoon
• Sour cream	2 cups
• Smoked salmon	8 slices, cut into strips (about 4 to 6 ounces)
• Fresh chives	2 tablespoons, minced
or	
• Chunky applesauce (instead of smoked salmon and chives)	2 cups

SPECIAL EQUIPMENT
16-inch pizza stone, wooden pizza peel

PREPARATION

1 Place a pizza stone in the middle of your oven and preheat to 450° F, at least 30 minutes.

2 Shape the dough according to the recipe on page 16. Work with only 1 piece of dough at a time, as your pizza stone may not accommodate more.

3 Peel and coarsely grate the potatoes. Place in a large mixing bowl along with the onion. Season with salt and pepper, and toss to mix. Work lightly, so that the strips of potato don't mash.

4 Cover the pizza dough with the potato mixture to within $\frac{1}{2}$ inch of the edge. Press down lightly, so that the potato layer is an even thickness. Drizzle with olive oil.

5 Transfer the pizza to the oven and bake for 5 to 8 minutes, or until the crust is golden brown and the potatoes look like well-done hash-browns. If preparing another pizza, do so while the first is in the oven.

6 Cut the pizza into sections. Top each with a dollop of sour cream and a strip of smoked salmon. Sprinkle with chives and serve. If not using smoked salmon and chives, serve the sour cream and apple sauce on the side.

christmas tree pizza

Makes 1 very large, 2 medium pizzas, or 4 individual pizzas

Decorate this pizza with your favorite "ornaments." If making individual pizzas, let the kids decorate their own.

SHOPPING/PANTRY/REFRIGERATOR LIST	HOW MUCH YOU'LL NEED
• Traditional or Honey-Wheat Pizza Dough (pages 14, 17)	1 pound
• Marinara/Pizza Sauce (page 21)	$\frac{1}{2}$ cup
• Mozzarella cheese	6 ounces, grated (2 cups)
• Fresh baby spinach leaves	2 cups
• Baby arugula leaves	2 cups
• Fresh basil leaves	1 cup
• Cherry or pearl tomatoes	1 cup halved
• Grated Parmesan cheese	3 tablespoons

SPECIAL EQUIPMENT
16-inch pizza stone, wooden pizza peel

PREPARATION

1 Place a seasoned (or oiled) pizza stone in the middle of your oven and preheat to 450° F, at least 30 minutes.

2 If making more than 1 pizza, divide the dough into 2 or 4 pieces, then roll and shape each piece into a tall triangle. These pizzas will be decorated after baking, so prepare all of them at once.

3 Spread the sauce over the dough to within 1 inch of the outer edge. Top that with mozzarella, transfer to the oven, and bake for 5 to 10 minutes, or until the cheese is melted and bubbly.

4 Meanwhile, combine the spinach, arugula, and basil leaves in a large bowl. When the pizzas are cooked, place them on serving platters and allow them to cool slightly. Top with overlapping leaves, making sure that the 3 different types are evenly distributed.

5 Cover the leaves with tomato halves, cut side down, and sprinkle with Parmesan "snow" before serving.

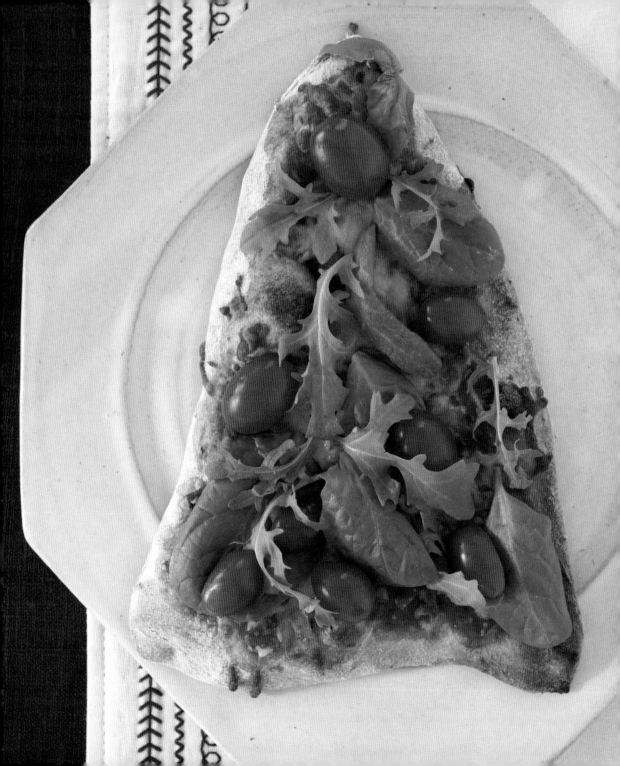

pizza for the holidays

Makes one 13-inch pizza or two 9-inch pizzas

Everyone has a favorite way to use holiday leftovers. This pizza may just cause you to think about making your holiday specialties all year round! For your repertoire . . .

SHOPPING/PANTRY/REFRIGERATOR LIST
- Traditional or Honey-Wheat Pizza Dough (pages 14, 17)
- Mashed potatoes, au gratin potatoes, or stuffing
- Mozzarella cheese, plain or smoked
- Roasted or smoked turkey strips
  or
- Glazed or smoked ham
- Cranberry sauce or relish (preferably homemade)

HOW MUCH YOU'LL NEED
1 pound

2 cups

3 ounces, grated (1 cup)
2 cups, cubed or cut into strips

2 cups, cubed or cut into strips
2 cups

SPECIAL EQUIPMENT
16-inch pizza stone, wooden pizza peel

PREPARATION

1 Place a seasoned (or oiled) pizza stone in the middle of your oven and preheat to 450° F, at least 30 minutes.

2 Roll and shape the dough into one 13-inch or two 9-inch circles and place on a floured pizza peel (see page 18 for instructions on handling and shaping pizza dough). If you are more comfortable working with one piece of dough at a time, you can shape and dress the second piece while the first is in the oven. If making 2 pizzas, split all the topping ingredients in half.

3 Whether using potatoes or stuffing, make sure that the topping is at room temperature and spreadable so that you won't tear the dough. Spread the topping of your choice over the dough to within 1 inch of the dough's edge.

4 Distribute the mozzarella over the top of the pizza.

5 Cover the cheese with the meat of your choice and transfer the pizza to the oven.

6 Bake for 8 to 10 minutes, or until the crust is golden brown and the cheese is melted and bubbly. Slice and serve with cranberry sauce or relish.

dessert pizzas

With every CPKids tour of one of our restaurants, there is at least one kid who wants to turn his or her favorite dessert into a pizza. Who can blame them? Both pizza and dessert are fun to make and to eat; why not combine the two? Here are a few recipes that will, we hope, inspire you to do just that.

warm apple pie pizza

Makes one 13-inch pizza, two 9-inch pizzas, or four 6-inch pizzas

Top this one with a scoop of vanilla ice cream!

SHOPPING/PANTRY/REFRIGERATOR LIST	HOW MUCH YOU'LL NEED
• Light brown sugar	½ cup firmly packed
• All-purpose flour	½ cup
• Ground cinnamon	¼ teaspoon
• Kosher salt	Pinch
• Unsalted butter	2 tablespoons, very cold
• Neapolitan Pizza Dough (page 16)	14 ounces
• Light corn syrup	1 teaspoon
• Water	¼ teaspoon
• Granny Smith apple	1 large, peeled, cored, and thinly sliced

SPECIAL EQUIPMENT
16-inch pizza stone, wooden pizza peel, 1-inch pastry brush

PREPARATION

1 Place a seasoned (or oiled) pizza stone in the middle of your oven and preheat to 450° F, at least 30 minutes.

2 Combine the brown sugar, flour, cinnamon, and salt in a large mixing bowl and blend with your hands. Don't worry if there are small lumps of brown sugar; they will melt during baking. Cut the butter into tiny cubes and add to the bowl. Blend the butter in with your fingertips, working just until there are no chunks of butter visible.

3 Shape the dough according to the recipe on page 16 (if making more than one pizza, try to make them at the same time). Combine the corn syrup with ¼ teaspoon water and brush this mixture on the outer inch of the dough.

4 Arrange the apple slices in a pinwheel pattern over the dough (do not overlap the slices), and cover the entire surface with the brown sugar mixture.

5 Transfer to the oven and bake for 7 to 10 minutes, or until the crust and topping are nicely browned. Remove from the oven, slice, and serve immediately.

s'mores "pizza"

Makes one 10- or 11-inch "pizza"

The next-best thing to the campfire favorite.

SHOPPING/PANTRY/REFRIGERATOR LIST
- Graham cracker crumbs
- Unsalted butter
- Light brown sugar
- Semi-sweet chocolate chips
- Mini marshmallows

HOW MUCH YOU'LL NEED
$1\frac{1}{2}$ cups
4 tablespoons ($\frac{1}{2}$ stick), melted
2 tablespoons packed
1 (twelve-ounce) bag (2 cups)
2 cups

SPECIAL EQUIPMENT
10- or 11-inch removable-bottom tart pan

PREPARATION

1 Preheat the oven to 375° F. Lightly grease a removable-bottom tart pan with butter, oil, or cooking spray.

2 Combine the graham cracker crumbs, butter, and brown sugar in a small bowl; mix evenly. Press the crumb mixture evenly into the bottom and halfway up the rim of the assembled pan. Cover the crust with an even layer of chocolate chips and cover those with the marshmallows.

3 Bake for 15 to 20 minutes, or until the marshmallows are melted and golden brown. Remove the pizza and cool on a wire rack for 5 minutes. Then, carefully remove the tart ring. Slice and serve.

dessert "pizza"

Makes one 13-inch pizza, two 9-inch pizzas, or four 6-inch pizzas

Be sure to cut the pizza as soon as it comes out of the oven, before topping it. You'll need a pie server to transfer the portions to serving plates.

SHOPPING/PANTRY/REFRIGERATOR LIST	HOW MUCH YOU'LL NEED
• Traditional or Honey-Wheat Pizza Dough (pages 14, 17) or	1 pound
• Neapolitan Pizza Dough (page 16)	14 ounces
• Confectioners' sugar	1/4 cup
• Toppings (see below)	Sky's the limit

SPECIAL EQUIPMENT
16-inch pizza stone, wooden pizza peel, mesh strainer

PREPARATION

1 Place a seasoned (or oiled) pizza stone in the middle of your oven and preheat to 450° F, at least 30 minutes.

2 Roll and shape the dough into one 13-inch, two 9-inch, or four 6-inch circles and place on a floured pizza peel (see page 18 for instructions on handling and shaping pizza dough). If making 6-inch pizzas, prepare 2 at a time.

3 Place the sugar in a fine-mesh strainer and cover the dough with a thin, even layer of sugar. This will caramelize as the pizza bakes.

4 Transfer the pizza to the oven and bake for 5 to 10 minutes, depending on the thickness of the dough. The crust should be golden brown and thoroughly cooked. Use the peel or 2 broad spatulas to remove the crust(s), and place on individual serving plates or a serving platter. Cut the crusts into desired portions. (Tip: let everyone top his or her own individual pizza.)

5 Top the crust(s) while still warm with any or all of the following (caution: this is not an exhaustive list!).

DESSERT "PIZZA" TOPPINGS
Whipped cream, ice cream (1 scoop per serving), chocolate sauce, caramel sauce, strawberry sauce, chopped toasted nuts, chocolate chips (semi-sweet or white), M&Ms, jelly beans, sliced bananas, sliced strawberries, raspberries, blackberries, and/or blueberries, crushed cookies, jimmies, toasted coconut, gummy bears, chopped toffee pieces, Reese's Pieces

dessert "pizza" on a cookie

Makes one 10- or 11-inch "pizza"—about 12 servings

Make this pizza when you don't have the time to prepare pizza dough.

SHOPPING/PANTRY/REFRIGERATOR LIST
- Sugar cookie dough (homemade or storebought)
- Toppings (see page 111)

HOW MUCH YOU'LL NEED
1 pound at room temperature

Sky's the limit!

SPECIAL EQUIPMENT
10- or 11-inch removable-bottom tart pan

PREPARATION

1 Preheat the oven to 375° F. Lightly grease a removable-bottom tart pan with butter, oil, or cooking spray.

2 Press the dough evenly into the bottom of the assembled pan. There is no need to go up the rim; the dough will form a rim during baking. Bake the crust for 15 to 20 minutes, or until it is light brown and just becoming firm.

3 Remove the crust and cool on a wire rack for 5 minutes. Then, carefully remove the tart ring. Carefully loosen the crust from the tart bottom and transfer to a serving platter. Cut the crust, which should still be warm and somewhat soft, into desired portions.

4 Top as you would the Dessert "Pizza" on page 111.

faux mushroom-pepperoni pizza

Makes one 13-inch pizza, two 9-inch pizzas, or four 6-inch pizzas

Pizza for dessert? Not exactly.

SHOPPING/PANTRY/REFRIGERATOR LIST
- Traditional or Honey-Wheat Pizza Dough (pages 14, 17)
- Strawberry jam
- Flaked coconut
- Strawberry or cherry fruit leather
- Marshmallows

HOW MUCH YOU'LL NEED
1 pound

$\frac{1}{2}$ cup
1 cup
4 strips
6, snipped in half

SPECIAL EQUIPMENT
16-inch pizza stone, wooden pizza peel

PREPARATION

1 Place a seasoned (or oiled) pizza stone in the middle of your oven and preheat to 450° F, at least 30 minutes.

2 Roll and shape the dough into one 13-inch, two 9-inch, or four 6-inch circles and place on a floured pizza peel (see page 18 for instructions on handling and shaping pizza dough). If making 6-inch pizzas, prepare 2 at a time.

3 Spread a thin layer of jam ("sauce") to within 1 inch of the outer edge of the dough. Cover the sauce with an even layer of coconut ("cheese"), spreading it to within $\frac{1}{2}$ inch of the edge of the dough.

4 Using a 1- or 1$\frac{1}{4}$-inch plain round cookie cutter, cut rounds of fruit leather and distribute them over the pizza (for the "pepperoni"). Distribute the marshmallow "mushrooms" over the pizza, making sure that some of the fruit leather shows.

5 Transfer to the heated pizza stone and bake for 5 to 7 minutes, or until the crust and marshmallows are lightly browned. Remove from the oven, slice, and serve.

toppings, garnishes, and things that go crunch

Combining different textures and flavors is the key to making a pizza or salad exciting. Here are a few "building blocks" that will make your creations stand up tall.

candied walnuts

Makes about 3 cups

Candied Walnuts will keep for up to 1 week in an airtight container at room temperature. Do not refrigerate, as the moisture from your refrigerator will melt the caramel.

SHOPPING/PANTRY/REFRIGERATOR LIST
- Honey
- Sugar
- Unsalted butter
- Walnut halves and pieces
- Kosher salt

HOW MUCH YOU'LL NEED
3 tablespoons
6 tablespoons
4 tablespoons ($\frac{1}{2}$ stick)
$2\frac{1}{2}$ cups (about 12 ounces)
Pinch

PREPARATION

1 Preheat the oven to 350° F. Lightly grease a cookie sheet with nonstick cooking spray or butter.

2 Combine the honey, 3 tablespoons of the sugar, and the butter in a large nonstick frying pan and heat, stirring constantly, until the mixture begins to boil. Lower the heat and simmer the mixture, stirring occasionally, until it is syrupy and light beige in color, 2 to 3 minutes. Turn off the heat.

3 Add the walnuts to the syrup and stir to coat them completely. Transfer the nuts to the cookie sheet and spread them evenly. Bake for 12 to 15 minutes, turning the pan once. They should be a deep caramel color.

4 Carefully remove the walnuts to a mixing bowl, scraping any bits that stick to the pan with a metal spatula. Sprinkle the nuts with the remaining 3 tablespoons sugar and the salt. Toss to coat evenly. Allow the nuts to cool completely before storing.

crisp rice sticks or fried wonton strips

Makes 2 cups rice sticks or 3 cups wonton strips

You'll find rice sticks and wonton wrappers in Asian markets and in the Asian specialty section of many supermarkets.

....

SHOPPING/PANTRY/REFRIGERATOR LIST	HOW MUCH YOU'LL NEED
Canola oil	1 quart
Rice sticks (fine)	2 ounces (1 bundle)
Wonton wrappers	1 package

....

SPECIAL EQUIPMENT
Candy or oil thermometer, wire skimmer

PREPARATION

1 Heat the oil to 400° F in a large, deep pot.

2 While the oil is heating, gently unfold the bundle of rice sticks and spread them apart. Don't worry if some of the pieces break; they can still be fried. Cut wonton wrappers into ¼-inch strips and toss to separate the pieces.

3 When the oil is hot, place all of the rice sticks in the pan, pressing down gently with the wire skimmer (if they won't all fit, then fry half at a time). They will puff immediately. Fry for about 5 seconds. Fry wonton strips for about 30 seconds, or until golden.

4 Remove immediately with the wire skimmer, and drain on several layers of paper towels. Allow the rice sticks or wonton strips to cool.

5 Gently crush the fried rice sticks with your hands. Store either topping at room temperature in an airtight container for up to 24 hours.

greek salad

Makes 3 cups

SHOPPING/PANTRY/REFRIGERATOR LIST

- English (hothouse) cucumber
- Roma tomatoes
- Red onion
- Pitted kalamata olives
- Lemon juice
- Red wine vinegar
- Sugar
- Garlic
- Dried oregano leaves
- Kosher salt
- Ground black pepper
- Extra-virgin olive oil

HOW MUCH YOU'LL NEED

1 large or 2 small, peeled and diced $^3/_8$ inch
2 medium, seeded and diced $^3/_8$ inch
1 medium, chopped
$^1/_2$ cup, drained and halved lengthwise
1 teaspoon
1 teaspoon
$^1/_2$ teaspoon
$^1/_4$ teaspoon, minced
Pinch
Pinch
Pinch
1 tablespoon

PREPARATION

1 Combine the cucumber, tomatoes, onion, and olives in a large mixing bowl.

2 Whisk together the remaining ingredients in a small bowl and add to the vegetables. Stir well.

3 Use immediately, or store in the refrigerator for up to 24 hours.

grilled vegetables

Makes about 3 cups asparagus; 2 cups zucchini, eggplant, or peppers; about 1 cup scallions

Use any or all of these to top a pizza or in the Grilled Vegetable Salad (page 36). Make them when you're grilling other foods; they'll keep in the refrigerator for up to 3 days.

SHOPPING/PANTRY/REFRIGERATOR LIST	HOW MUCH YOU'LL NEED
• Asparagus	2 bunches (about 1 pound)
• Olive oil	1 to 2 tablespoons per vegetable
• Kosher salt	1 teaspoon per vegetable
• Ground black pepper	$\frac{1}{2}$ teaspoon per vegetable
• Zucchini	3 large (about 1 pound)
• Japanese eggplant	3 large (about 1 pound)
• Red bell peppers	2 large
• Yellow bell peppers	2 large
• Scallions (green onions)	3 bunches

SPECIAL EQUIPMENT
1-inch pastry brush, hot grill

PREPARATION

1 Cut the bottom 2 to 3 inches off the asparagus spears and discard; blanch asparagus in boiling water for 20 seconds; remove immediately and cool in an ice-water bath. Once cool, drain the asparagus, pat dry, brush with olive oil, and sprinkle with salt and pepper.

2 Cut the stem ends off the zucchini and eggplant, then cut the vegetables lengthwise into ¼-inch inch-thick slices. Lay the slices on a cookie sheet and brush lightly—but thoroughly—with olive oil. Sprinkle with salt and pepper. Turn the slices and repeat.

3 Cut the tops off the bell peppers and remove the seeds. Cut the peppers lengthwise into quarters. With your knife parallel to the cutting board, cut away the pale-colored membranes. Brush both sides of the pepper quarters with olive oil, but sprinkle only the insides with salt and pepper.

4 Cut away the roots and the top 2 inches from the scallions. Remove the outermost leaf layer from each. Brush the scallions lightly with olive oil, then sprinkle with salt and pepper.

5 Heat a charcoal or gas grill.

6 Grill the zucchini and eggplant for about 2 minutes on each side, or until well marked and quite tender (you may not need to leave them for the full 2 minutes on the second side). Use tongs or a grilling spatula to remove the vegetables to a large platter or cookie sheet.

7 Grill the peppers for about 3 minutes on the skin side, or until the skin is just beginning to blister. Turn and grill for an additional 2 minutes, or until the peppers are quite flexible.

8 Grill the asparagus and scallions for about 3 minutes total, rolling them as you do so, to ensure even browning.

9 Once cooled, cut the asparagus, zucchini, eggplant, and scallions diagonally into 1-inch pieces. Peel any blackened skin from the peppers. Leave peppers in quarters (for panini) or cut into 1-inch diamonds (for salads or pizzas). Store the vegetables separately in the refrigerator for up to 3 days.

sautéed white mushrooms

Makes about ³/₄ cup

SHOPPING/PANTRY/REFRIGERATOR LIST
- White mushrooms
- Olive oil
- Kosher salt
- Ground black pepper

HOW MUCH YOU'LL NEED
8 ounces (¹/₂ pound)
1¹/₂ tablespoons
¹/₄ teaspoon
¹/₄ teaspoon

PREPARATION

1 Wash, dry, and trim the mushrooms. Slice them ¹/₄ inch thick.

2 Heat the oil in a skillet over high heat until it begins to smoke. Add the mushrooms and toss to coat them with oil.

3 Lower the heat slightly and cook the mushrooms, stirring occasionally, until all of the liquid has evaporated and the edges begin to brown, 9 to 10 minutes.

4 Turn off the heat and sprinkle the mushrooms evenly with salt and pepper.

5 Use immediately, or cool and refrigerate for up to 3 days.

index

A

Anaheim chiles, in chipotle chicken pizza, 81–82

Añejo enchilado cheese, in chipotle chicken pizza, 81–82

Apple(s)
  in Waldorf chicken salad, 42
  warm apple pie pizza, 107

Applesauce, in potato pancake pizza, 99

Arugula
  in chicken Milanese, 56–58
  in Christmas tree pizza, 100
  in vegetarian panini, 50–52

Asparagus
  grilled, 120
  in grilled vegetable salad, 36

Avocado
  club egg rolls, 25
  in grilled vegetable salad, 36
  in miso salad with crab and shrimp, 33
  in Thai crunch salad, 39–40
  in turkey club panini, 49

B

Bacon
  in avocado club egg rolls, 25–26
  in create-your-own pizza, 88
  honey-Dijon chicken and bacon panini, 46
  in Jamaican jerk chicken pizza, 68
  in turkey club panini, 49
  white pizza with, 77

Basil, in Christmas tree pizza, 100

Beans, black, in chipotle salsa, 83

Beef, hamburger meat, in create-your-own pizza, 88

Bell peppers
  green, in "the works" pizza, 78
  grilled, 120
  yellow, in vegetarian panini, 50–52

Blueberries, in Fourth of July pizza, 92

Broccolini, in vegetarian pizza with Japanese eggplant and goat cheese, 71–73

C

Cabbage
  in miso salad with crab and shrimp, 33
  in Thai crunch salad, 39–40

Candy
  corn, in Halloween jack-o-lantern pizza, 95
  in dessert "pizza," 111

Caramel sauce, in dessert "pizza," 111

Caribbean sauce, 70

Carrots
  in miso salad with crab and shrimp, 33
  in orange chicken lettuce wraps, 30
  in Thai crunch salad, 39–40

Celery, in Waldorf chicken salad, 42

Checca, 58

Cheese
  curly mac & cheese, 55
  See also Añejo enchilado cheese; Feta cheese; Fontina cheese; Goat cheese; Gorgonzola cheese; Monterey Jack cheese; Parmesan cheese; Ricotta cheese; Romano cheese; Swiss cheese

Chicken
  grilled
    in avocado club egg rolls, 25–26
  grilled garlic
    in chipotle chicken pizza, 81–82
    in grilled chicken pesto panini, 45

F

Faux mushroom-pepperoni pizza, 111
Feta cheese
 in Greek pizza, 65–67
 in tzatziki sauce, 67
Fontina cheese
 in Sicilian pizza, 74
 in white pizza with bacon, 77
Food processor, over-kneading, avoiding, 14
Fourth of July pizza, 92
Fruit
 in dessert "pizza," 111
 dessert "pizza" on a cookie, 112
 See also Blueberries; Strawberries
Fruit leather, in faux mushroom-pepperoni pizza, 111
Fusilli, in curly mac & cheese, 55

G

Garlic chicken. See Chicken, grilled garlic
Goat cheese, vegetarian pizza with Japanese eggplant
 and
Gorgonzola cheese, in Waldorf chicken salad, 42
Grapes, in Waldorf chicken salad, 42
Greek chicken, grilled
 in Greek pizza, 65–67
 recipe, 22
Greek salad, 119
Grilled chicken. See Chicken, grilled
Grilled vegetables
 grilled vegetable salad, 36
 recipe, 120

H

Halloween jack-o-lantern pizza, 95
Ham
 capocolio, in Sicilian pizza, 74
 in pizza for the holidays, 103

Hand-mixing, dough, 14
Honey-Dijon chicken and bacon panini, 46
Honey-wheat pizza dough, 17
Hot dogs, in create-your-own pizza, 88

I

Ice cream
 in dessert "pizza," 111
 in Fourth of July pizza, 92
 in Valentine's Day pizza, 91

J

Jamaican jerk chicken, grilled
 in Jamaican jerk chicken pizza, 68
 recipe, 22
Japanese eggplant
 grilled, 120
 in grilled vegetable salad, 36
 vegetarian pizza and goat cheese with, 71–73

L

Lemon(s), in piccata cream sauce, 64
Lettuce wraps
 with chicken, 27
 lettuce wrap sauce, 29
 orange chicken, 30
Lime
 -cilantro dressing, 39
 cream sauce, 83
Linguini, chicken Marsala with, 59–61

M

Marinara/pizza sauce
 basic recipe, 21
 spicy, 21
Marsala sauce, 61

R

Raspberries
    in Fourth of July pizza, 92
    in Valentine's Day pizza, 91
Rice sticks, 118
Ricotta cheese, in white pizza with bacon, 77
Roasted peppers, in Jamaican jerk chicken pizza, 68
Romaine lettuce, in grilled vegetable salad, 36
Romano cheese, in white pizza with bacon, 77

S

Safety in kitchen, 11
Salad(s)
    Greek, 119
    Thai crunch, 39–40
    vegetable, grilled, 36
    Waldorf chicken, 42
Salami, Italian, in Sicilian pizza, 74
Salmon, smoked, in potato pancake pizza, 99
Sauce(s)
    Caribbean, 70
    cipotle salsa, 83
    lettuce wrap, 29
    lime cream, 82
    marinara/pizza sauce, 21
    Marsala, 61
    piccata cream, 64
    Szechuan orange, 32
    tzatziki, 67
Sausage
    cpkids' pizza with mushroom, pepperoni and, 87
    in create-your-own pizza, 88
    in Sicilian pizza, 74
    in "the works" pizza, 78
Scallion(s)
    grilled, 120
    in grilled vegetable salad, 36
    in Jamaican jerk chicken pizza, 68
    in lettuce wraps with chicken, 27
    in miso salad with crab and shrimp, 33
    in orange chicken lettuce wraps, 30
    in Thai crunch salad, 39–40
Shallot(s), in lime cream sauce, 82
Shitake mushrooms
    in lettuce wraps with chicken, 27
    in orange chicken lettuce wraps, 30
Shrimp, miso salad with shrimp and, 33
Sicilian pizza, 74
S'mores pizza, 108
Sour cream
    in lime cream sauce, 82
    in potato pancake pizza, 99
    in tzatziki sauce, 67
Spicy marinara sauce, 21
Spinach
    in Christmas tree pizza, 100
    in white pizza with bacon, 77
Strawberries, in Valentine's Day pizza, 91
Strawberry jam, in faux mushroom-pepperoni pizza, 115
Sweet potatoes, Thanksgiving sweet potato pizza, 96
Swiss cheese, in create-your-own pizza, 88
Szechuan orange sauce, 32

T

Thai crunch salad, 39–40
Thai peanut dressing, 41
Thanksgiving sweet potato pizza, 96
Thin crust (Neapolitan) pizza dough, 16–17
Tomato(es)
    in avocado club egg rolls, 25–26
    in checca, 58
    cherry, in Christmas tree pizza, 100
    in chipotle salsa, 83
    in Greek salad, 119
    sun-dried
        in grilled vegetable salad, 36